THE SIEGE OF LENINGRAD

THEN AND NOW

THE SIEGE OF LENINGRAD
THEN AND NOW

Edited by Daniel Taylor

An Imprint of Pen & Sword Books Ltd

The Siege of Leningrad Then and Now
© *After the Battle* and Daniel Taylor, 2024

Published by After the Battle
An imprint of Pen & Sword Books Ltd
47 Church Street, Barnsley,
South Yorkshire, S70 2AS
Tel. 01226 734222
Fax. 01226 734438
Email: enquiries@pen-and-sword.co.uk
Website: **www.afterthebattle.com**
   www.pen-and-sword.co.uk

Printed and bound in India by Replika Press Pvt. Ltd.

ISBN: 9781399031165

Commissioning Editor: Rob Green
Editor: Daniel Taylor
Design: Paul Wilkinson
Cover design: Jon Wilkinson

Credits:
This book is based on an article originally published in *After the Battle Magazine*:
'The Siege of Leningrad' by Karel Margry & Ron Hogg (February 2004)

Acknowledgements:
Clearly the original work carried out by Ron Hogg, crafted by *After the Battle*'s longstanding former Editor, Karel Margry are fundamental to the creation of this book. I would also like to thank Rob Green, *After the Battle*'s Commissioning Editor for giving me the opportunity to recraft the work for a new audience. Freed from the limitations of producing the account within the tight limitations of the magazine, we have been able to incorporate a number of images collected for the article but never used - and to incorporate some stories that were beyond the remit of the original. Also intrinsic to the creation of the original articles were Vladimir Skvortsov and Tatiana Yeliseyeva. We are, as usual, inordinately grateful to Jon and Paul Wilkinson for their design work, respectively creating the cover and the interior layout for this book. I would also like to thank my able team of proof readers, James Snelling, Madeline Budgen and Joe Taylor.

Photo Credits
Front Cover: The monument created to commemorate the conquest of one foreign dictator is used to evoke passion for the defeat of another. The Narva Gate celebrated victory over Napoleon in the war of 1812 and volunteers from the Kirov metallurgical plant parade for the camera. Visiting the site today, the Gate is on Stachek Square which leads straight to the Kirov factory.

Back Cover:
Upper Left: A frequent night-time scene in besieged Leningrad, this battery of 85mm 52K anti-aircraft guns engage a German night incusion. They are situated in Ploschad Dekabristov (Decembrists Square) with the dome of St Isaac's Cathedral silhouetted in the background.

Lower Left: A more peaceful scene in front of the cathedral pictured in 2003.

Upper Right: Every scrap of public space was turned over to food production. A healthy crop of cabbages is ready for harvesting on St Isaac's Square.

Lower Right: The same place today, now overlooked by the Astoria Hotel.

Bottom: Another 85mm 52-K dug in on Marsovo Pole (Field of Mars).

CONTENTS

FOREWORD 6
LENINGRAD 8
OPERATION 'BARBAROSSA' 10
LENINGRAD PREPARES FOR SIEGE 13
RENEWED GERMAN OFFENSIVE 25
THE BALTIC FLEET WITHDRAWS TO LENINGRAD 28
LENINGRAD ISOLATED 29
THE FINNS CLOSE THE RING FROM THE NORTH 36
BEGINNING OF THE SIEGE 38
WINTER 1941-42 53
THE 'ROAD OF LIFE' – ACROSS LAKE LADOGA 63
1942: FAILED ATTEMPTS TO LIFT THE SIEGE 77
1943: THE BLOCKADE IS BROKEN 86
1944: END OF THE SIEGE 90
CONCLUSION 95

A German machine gun nest set up to fire on fixed lines during the summer of 1942. The flat open countryside exemplifies the terrain south and southwest of the city. SSETO

FOREWORD

AS A SYMBOL of perseverance and forbearance there can be few better examples than the cataclysmic siege endured by the populace of Leningrad between August 1941 and January 1944. The horrors of a city of three and half million souls, cut off from almost all means of supply, can scarcely be imagined.

Despite the prolonged siege, many of Leningrad's streets, monuments and buildings remained recognisable and relatively intact. Although the city was surrounded and subject to artillery and aerial attack, the fact that the invading army did not enter the town, limited the extent to which neighbourhoods were pulverised and so this offers an opportunity for *After the Battle*'s unique format to take a comparative look, both then and now.

The siege offers a peculiar insight into the Russian psyche, in particular that of the county's current president, Vladimir Putin. Born in Leningrad eight years after the war, Putin's outlook can be attributed to his formative years in the city, which still bore the fresh scars of the conflict. His parents lived through the siege and his brother, Viktor, died from starvation in it, aged just one year old. The siege of Leningrad remains a prominent part of the Russian educational curriculum and it is widely used in the country's perception of itself. It is a symbol of fortitude in adversity and consequently one of the attributes that many Russians admire most is the ability to endure hardship patiently, confident in the knowledge that their resolve will outmatch their opponent.

Naming Conventions

Where military units are named, it is *After the Battle*'s practice to represent them as they originally appear in the documents of their respective countries. With Russian units the use of Cyrillic script clearly makes this difficult and so suitable English titles are employed as this still presents a differentiation with the opposing German forces. German spellings are used for all their groupings. Where specific numbers are used to refer to units, the German use of a full-stop is employed, roughly equating to the ordinals in English numbering (ie the 'th' after a number). This convention has been set aside when describing corps level German units, where Roman numerals appear, as the proliferation of full-stops became distracting, without adding clarification. The opposing hierarchy therefore appears as follows (the specific units named are examples only):

Part of the Monument to the Heroic Defenders of Leningrad. This extensive and impressive sculpture is composed of ten such sculptural vignettes and sits atop a commemorative subterranean museum. It is the centrepiece of Ploschad Pobedy (Victory Square), lying in the middle of a large roundabout on the road leading into St. Petersburg from its international airport.

German	**Russian**	**Classification**
Heeresgruppe Nord	North-Western Front	Army Group
18. Armee	11th Army	Army
LVI Panzerkorps	CX Rifle Corps	Corps
3. Infanterie-Division	1st (Kirov) Division	Division

LENINGRAD

NESTLED BETWEEN LAKE LADOGA to the east and the Gulf of Finland to the West, Leningrad is largely situated across a number of islands in the mouth of the River Neva, flowing between the two bodies of water. The terrain is low lying, swampy and boasts a severe climate. Historically, the area had been inhabited by the Swedes but was conquered by Russia during the Great Northern War (1700-21) fought between Sweden and a coalition of countries led by Russia. In 1703, Russian Tsar Peter the Great chose a site on Zayachiy (Hare) Island by the Neva to build a defensive fortress and eventually a new city was constructed to be a 'window on the West' for the country. At first only a crude earthwork, the fortress was replaced between 1706 and 1725 by a new four-metre-thick, brick wall construction. Later a granite slab facing was added. Known as the Peter and Paul Fortress, it housed the city's first prison and a cathedral with a beautiful soaring spire 122 metres high (which was to make an excellent artillery reference point for future invading forces). Construction of the fortress was followed by the construction of the Kronstadt naval base on one of the Neva delta islands, 15 miles to the west of the city and then attention was given to the construction of the many splendid palaces, wide boulevards, grandiose squares, and elegant canal and river bridges, which deliberately set out to evoke comparisons with other great cities such as Venice and Paris.

Peter the Great took up residence in the city in 1712 and for two centuries St Petersburg was the capital of the Tsarist Empire. In August 1914, at the start of World War I, the city renounced its Germanic-sounding name and became Petrograd, and as such it was the cradle of the revolutions that overthrew Tsarism and brought the Bolsheviks to power in October 1917. In 1918, the communists transferred the seat of government from Petrograd to Moscow. Five years later, in January 1924, they renamed the city 'Leningrad' in honour of Vladimir Ilyich Lenin, the revolutionary leader. Since 1991 the city has reverted to its pre-Soviet name of St Petersburg but in 1941 it was a thriving principal city of the Communist state.

Besides being a political and cultural centre and Russia's prime naval port, Leningrad was also an industrial hub. Prior to the blockade, industry in the city included over 520 factories producing armaments, chemicals, textiles, ships, diesel engines, machinery, machine tools and other items. The armaments factories were well established and had a long history of producing military equipment such as artillery, tanks and armoured cars, small arms and ammunition, artillery shells and chemicals.

Strategically and militarily, Leningrad was ill placed, located as it was on

This huge bronze statue of Lenin stands outside St. Petersburg's Finland Station. It was unveiled in 1926, completed three years after his death and shows him making a speech from the turret of an armoured car as he did soon after his arrival in the city in 1917. It was created by sculptor Sergei A. Evseev directed by the architects Vladimir Shchuko and Vladimir Helfreich.

the narrow Karelian Isthmus, hemmed in between the Gulf of Finland on its western side and the huge Ladoga Lake on its eastern side – the latter, one of the largest lakes in Europe – almost isolates the city from the rest of the country.

Leningraders possessed – and still possess today – a strong pride in their city, which they regard as the most sophisticated and outward looking of all Russian cities. They tend to look down somewhat on the rest of Russia and cherish a position of independence vis-à-vis Moscow.

Leningrad • 9

OPERATION 'BARBAROSSA'

Generalfeldmarschall Wilhelm Ritter von Leeb was one of the Wehrmacht's most experienced army commanders. After an illustrious record in the Great War, he had served with the Reichswehr in the inter-war period. At 63 years of age, he was also the second oldest German general after Gerd von Rundstedt. (SSETO)

ON 22ND JUNE, 1941, Germany began the invasion of the Soviet Union (Operation 'Barbarossa'). Three army groups attacked across a wide area from the Baltic to the Black Sea: on the left wing Heeresgruppe Nord began an advance along the Baltic coast towards Leningrad; in the centre Heeresgruppe Mitte made the main thrust aiming for Moscow; and on the right Heeresgruppe Süd pushed into Ukraine and the Don Basin.

Heeresgruppe Nord under Generalfeldmarschall Ritter von Leeb consisted of two infantry armies and one panzer army. In the line from north to south were the 18. Armee under Generaloberst Georg von Küchler with eight infantry divisions; Panzergruppe 4 under Generaloberst Erich Hoepner with three armoured and five infantry divisions; and the 16. Armee under Generaloberst Ernst Busch with ten infantry divisions. Counting follow-up divisions, von Leeb had under his command a force of half a million men in 30 divisions. He also had 430 aircraft available for operations. The mission of the northern army group was to destroy the enemy forces operating in the Baltic area and to capture Leningrad and the Kronstadt naval base. Hitler had given von Leeb a clear directive to raze the city of Leningrad and make it completely uninhabitable, thus avoiding having to divert resources to feed the population during the coming winter.

The army group had a long way to go, the distance from East Prussia to Leningrad being some 500 miles. Von Leeb's plan was to launch Hoepner's Panzergruppe 4 on a single concentrated panzer strike to Leningrad, protected on both flanks by the two infantry armies. For this task Hoepner had two armoured corps. Operating on the left would be the XXXXI Panzerkorps under Generaloberst Hans Reinhardt, comprising the 1. and 6. Panzer-Divisions, the 36. Infanterie-Division (mot.) and the 269. Infanterie-Division; on the right would be the LVI Panzerkorps under Generaloberst Erich von Manstein, with the 8. Panzer-Division, the 3. Infanterie-Division

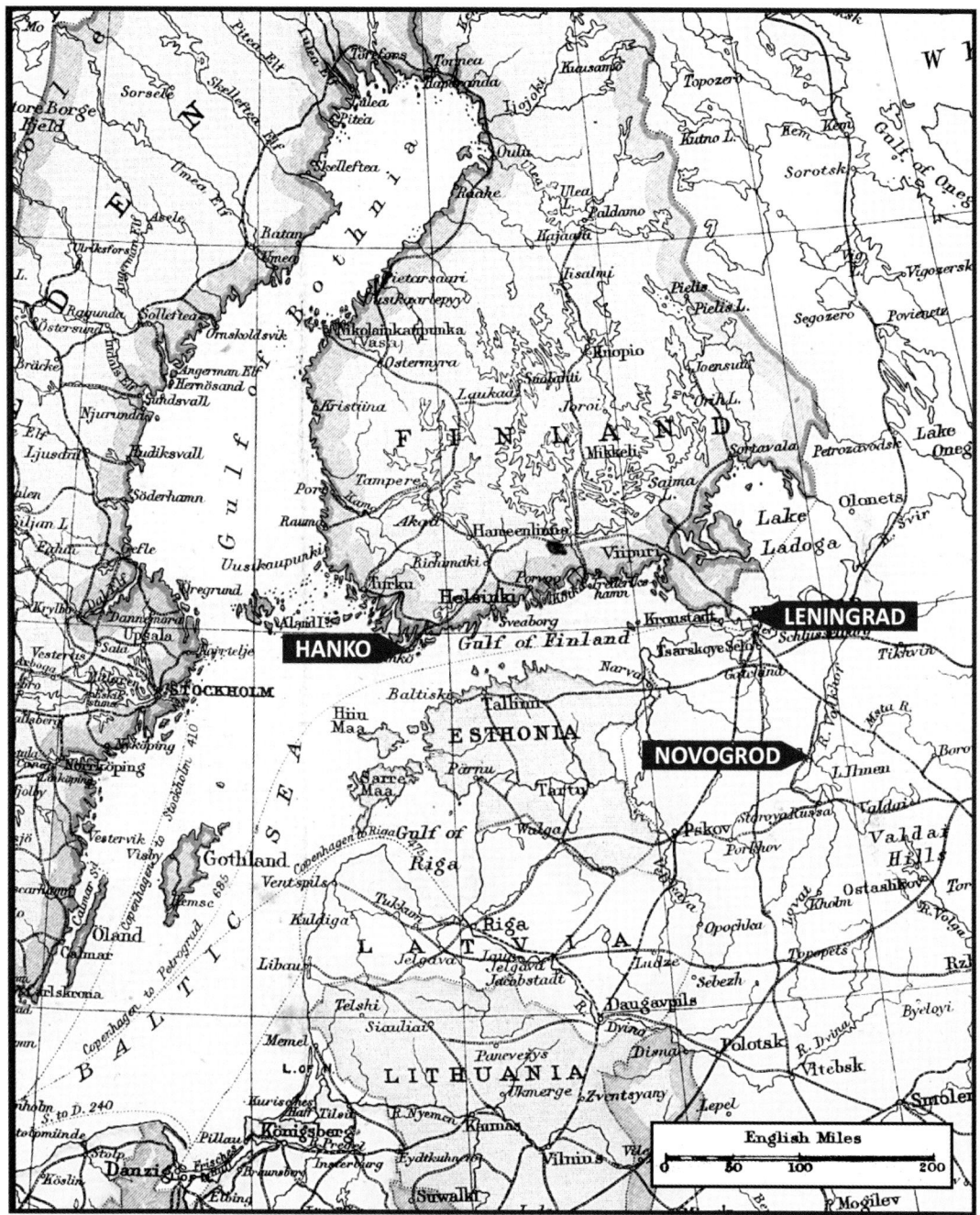

The siege of Leningrad was the longest ever endured by a modern city, and the deadliest siege in recorded history. It lasted for nearly 900 days, from late August 1941 to late January 1944, bringing unparalleled hardship to the population. Out of over three million civilians in the city more than one million lost their lives through cold, disease and starvation, bombs and artillery fire. The severe winter of 1941-42 was by far the worst period of the siege, when food reserves ran out, rations dropped to a little over 85 grams of bread per person per day and regular supplies of water, fuel, and electricity stopped. Its epic suffering and endurance earned Leningrad the title of 'Hero City of the Soviet Union'.

Though mechanised, Heeresgruppe Nord was still largely composed of foot-slogging infantry who had to march across Russia's vast expanse, across a dusty, landscape. (SSETO)

Colonel-General Fyodor Isidorovich Kuznetsov. (SSETO)

Lieutenant-General Markian M. Popov. (SSETO)

(mot.) and the 290. Infanterie-Division. In reserve would be the motorised SS-Totenkopf-Division.

Opposing Heeresgruppe Nord along the border was the Baltic Special Military District (renamed North-Western Front after the start of hostilities) commanded by Colonel-General F. I. Kuznetsov. His three armies – the 8th, 11th, and 27th – comprised 28 infantry divisions and three mechanised corps, with a strength of 1,000 tanks. Defending the territory around Leningrad was the Leningrad Military District (soon to be renamed Northern Front, then Leningrad Front) under Lieutenant-General Markian M. Popov, which included the 7th, 14th and 23rd Armies with a total of 15 divisions.

Starting out from East Prussia on 22nd June, Heeresgruppe Nord's panzer spearheads made rapid progress through Lithuania. Soviet forces defending the frontier or launching counter-attacks were overwhelmed or pushed back. By 30th June, the German tanks had covered 150 miles and secured bridgeheads over the Dvina river, the first major obstacle on the road to Leningrad, where they paused to regroup.

LENINGRAD PREPARES FOR SIEGE

MEANWHILE, LENINGRAD AWAITED its uncertain future. The defence of the city was led by a committee of three men: Lieutenant-General Markian M. Popov, commander of the Leningrad Front; Peter S. Popkov, the Mayor of Leningrad (his official function was Chairman of the Leningrad City Soviet); and Andrei A. Zhdanov, the chief of the Communist Party in Leningrad. Within this troika, Zhdanov was the most influential. A loyal supporter of Stalin, he had been party boss of Leningrad since 1934 and a full member of the Politburo, the ruling body of the Communist party, since 1939. Considered by many a likely candidate to succeed Stalin in the case of his death, he was one of the most powerful men in the Soviet Union.

Andrei A. Zhdanov, chief of the Communist Party in Leningrad. (SSETO)

The defence of Leningrad benefited from two factors. One was the unusually high degree of political organisation already existing in the city: about 200,000 of its inhabitants were members of the Communist Party and another 300,000 teenagers belonged to the Komsomol (Young Communist League). Also highly organised was a large proportion of the city's industrial workforce. Another factor was the fervent local patriotism among the ordinary citizens. There was a strong feeling among the populace that their city was in danger and must be defended at all costs.

On 27th June – five days after the start of the German invasion – the city Soviet issued a decree mobilising the entire population of men between 16 and 50 and women between 16 and 45 for defence work. A large part of the conscripted force was put to work constructing a triple ring of fortifications around the city. Unaccustomed to such hard work, lacking proper work clothes and shoes, and equipped with only the simplest of hand tools, an army of hundreds of thousands of men, women and teenagers worked in unbroken 12-hour shifts. Constantly improved, by early September, the three separate lines encompassed 630 miles of earth walls, 400 miles of anti-tank ditches, 185 miles of wooden abatis, 5,000 machine-gun nests and 370 miles of barbed-wire entanglements. At the same time, an

On 27th June 1941, five days after the start of the German invasion (Operation 'Barbarossa'), the Leningrad City Council Executive Committee mobilised every able-bodied citizen – men and women – to erect defensive works on the approaches and inside the city itself. These women are building a barricade on Moscow Prospect. This avenue, the largest in the southern district of Leningrad and leading straight to the heart of the metropolis, was the most likely point of entry of any German force trying to advance into the city. We are looking north, back toward the centre. (Novosti)

This story could not have been produced without the invaluable help of two native Leningraders, Vladimir Skvortsov and Tatiana Yeliseyeva. All present-day comparison photos were taken by Vladimir, ably assisted by Tatiana. Vladimir was born and raised in Leningrad while Tatiana, although born in the south of Russia, has spent most of her life in the city. Encouraged by Ron Hogg to look into the history of the blockade, they were able to readily identify many of the locations of the wartime pictures and in an excellent position to research the more difficult ones.

Defensive work within the city itself began in late July and accelerated on 2nd September when German forces reached the southern outskirts. Here, a civilian labour detail is converting a department store on Starinevski Prospect into a strong point. With its complex of deeply echeloned defences, incorporating trenches, pillboxes, bunkers, obstacles, and anti-artillery, anti-tank and anti-aircraft positions, Leningrad set new standards for the defence of a modern major city.

A perfect comparison taken by Vladimir in the summer of 2003.

Leningrad Prepares for Siege • 15

Also, in late June 1941, the city and Communist Party authorities formed the Narodnoye Opolcheni (People's Militia) to create additional military forces to defend the city. The volunteers were used to make up rifle divisions, machine-gun battalions, partisan battalions and armed workers' detachments. About 107,000 workers received military training during July and August 1941 while on the job, and then formed armed detachments on the basis of one company per factory shop or section. By 1st November, the Party had formed 123 such detachments comprising 15,460 worker-soldiers. Here, a workers detachment marches across Old Kalinkin Bridge, one of the city's oldest bridges crossing the Fontanka river. (Novosti)

The Fontanka is in fact a branch canal from the wide Neva river and circumvents the city centre to the south. The Old Kalinkin Bridge is the westernmost of the bridges connecting the centre with the southern parts of the city.

Volunteers from the Kirov metallurgical plant march past the Narva Gate, the triumphal arch commemorating the Russian victory over Napoleon in the war of 1812. This picture is one of many taken by Boris Kudoyarov, the only reporter to spend the entire period of the seige in Leningrad. A photographer/reporter for Komsomolskaya Pravda, Kudoyarov was sent to Leningrad from Moscow on the first day of 'Barbarossa' but, unable to travel by air, he went by train across Vologda, detouring around Lake Ladoga to reach the city. For the next two and a half years he lived and suffered with the inhabitants, photographing the fighting near the city and everyday life in the streets, factories, schools and homes. In all he took some 3,000 photographs, a unique pictorial testimony to the heroic defence of Leningrad and the suffering of its inhabitants. (Novosti)

elaborate networks of barricades, road-blocks, concealed pillboxes and strong points were built up in the city suburbs. Air raid shelters able to accommodate 918,000 people had been built and trenches for another 672,000.

At the same time, a large part of the male population of the city was mobilised into the so-called Opolcheni – Peoples Volunteer Militia. Zhdanov's call for volunteers to enlist in militias went out on 27th June. The population responded with great enthusiasm and zeal. Over 10,890 volunteers signed up for service on the first day of registration, 30th June. By 6th July, 100,000 had enlisted and the next day this total had reached 160,000, including 32,000 women, 20,000

The Narva Gate stands in Stachek Square, which is in fact a mile down the road from the Old Kalinkin Bridge seen in the previous pictures. The volunteer soldiers are on Stachek Prospect, which leads straight to the Kirov factory.

Leningrad Prepares for Siege • 17

Evacuees assembling in front of Moscow Railway Station on Ploschad Vosstania (Insurrection Square). Shortly after the start of the German invasion, the city authorities began evacuating women, children and the elderly to safer areas, but these early evacuations were badly handled. Once the Germans sealed off the city and winter set in, evacuation became much more difficult, although it never ceased altogether. Massive displacement of the population only became possible again in early 1942, and some one million people – about half of Leningrad's surviving citizens – were brought out during the spring and summer months.

Communists and 18,000 Young Communists. The original plans to form 15 Opolcheni divisions proved too ambitious, for to enlist so many male factory workers would mean a dangerous reduction of the city's industrial output. Nevertheless, between 5th and 19th July, four Opolcheni divisions were formed. Their preparation for battle occurred in great haste, chaos and improvisation. There was an acute shortage of weapons, no uniforms, insufficient time to properly train the militia, and few of the officers had any previous command experience.

The 1st (Kirov) Division of Volunteers – some 12,000 strong and named after the Kirov machinery plant from which many of its soldiers originated – had already left Leningrad on the 10th July, for the front line, just six days after it had been formed. Each man had been issued with hand grenades and Molotov cocktails, but there were not enough rifles for everyone. Machine guns, mortars and artillery were also in short supply. Many of

Vladimir's comparison was taken with his back to the station. The thin-spired metro station seen across Vosstania Square is a post-war building, having been opened in 1955.

the men had only a pick, shovel, axe or hunting knife as a weapon. Those without a weapon were instructed to pick one up from a casualty at the first opportunity. The other militia divisions soon followed.

In late June, the city authorities began the evacuation of women and young children from the threatened city. As seemed inevitable under such circumstances, lack of coordination, bureaucratic chaos and official incompetence played its part. Thousands of children were put on trains, but for some inexplicable reason the trains were sent south-west, to Pskov and Novgorod, straight towards the advancing German armies. Even after enemy air attacks on the trains had inflicted casualties among the children, the authorities senselessly carried on with the evacuation. Eventually, the children were brought back to Leningrad and new trains organised to send them off, this time to Kirov and Sverdlovsk. Even then many of the trains spent days waiting in marshalling yards. When the Germans closed the ring around Leningrad in early September, there were still some 400,000 children inside the city.

The authorities also undertook to evacuate elderly people from the city. The pensioners were seen as an unnecessary burden to the city's food reserves – 'useless mouths to feed'. Many did not want to leave, but the authorities forced them out. Their departure was equally mishandled. Many of their trains only got as far as Rybatskoye, just six miles outside the city, only to be stranded there for days on end before they could finally roll on. Evacuating the young and old had little effect on the total number of people to be fed, for their place was quickly taken by the thousands of refugees

Leningrad was a centre of Soviet tank production, both the Kirov and Izhora factories manufacturing tanks and armoured vehicles. Despite the worsening conditions, production continued through the autumn of 1941, 491 tanks rolling off the Kirov assembly lines alone before the end of the year. Here a KV-1 rumbles through the triumphal arch of the General Staff Building on Palace Square on its way to the front. The graffiti on the turret reads: 'We will defend the gains of the October revolution'. Evacuation of the tank factories to the Ural region began in August 1941, continuing up until the Germans closed the evacuation routes in September. Although not everything had been brought out, in due course the Kirov and Izhora factories resumed tank production at Cheliabinsk and Sverdlovsk in the Urals. Due to the blockade and the resulting shortage of raw materials, power cuts, and the decimation of the labour force, all production of fighting vehicles in Leningrad came to a standstill. (Novosti)

The General Staff Building arch, built to celebrate Russia's victory in the Napoleonic Wars, stands unchanged. Rising in the background is the Alexander Column, another memorial to the 1812 victory, with the Winter Palace behind.

streaming into the city from towns and villages threatened by the German onslaught.

At the same time, following Stalin's decree to save the country's industry, plants and workshops were being evacuated to the Russian hinterland. Entire factories were dismantled, their machines and tools put on trains and despatched to the East. Here again, many trains did not make it and ended up marooned in various marshalling yards, leaving the industrial equipment to rust.

Measures were also taken to protect the city's numerous works of art. Statues and sculptures in squares and parks were sandbagged and clad with protective shuttering. The priceless treasures of the Hermitage Museum were packed in crates and shipped to Sverdlovsk.

Though the city was now a hub of feverish activity, the war itself initially

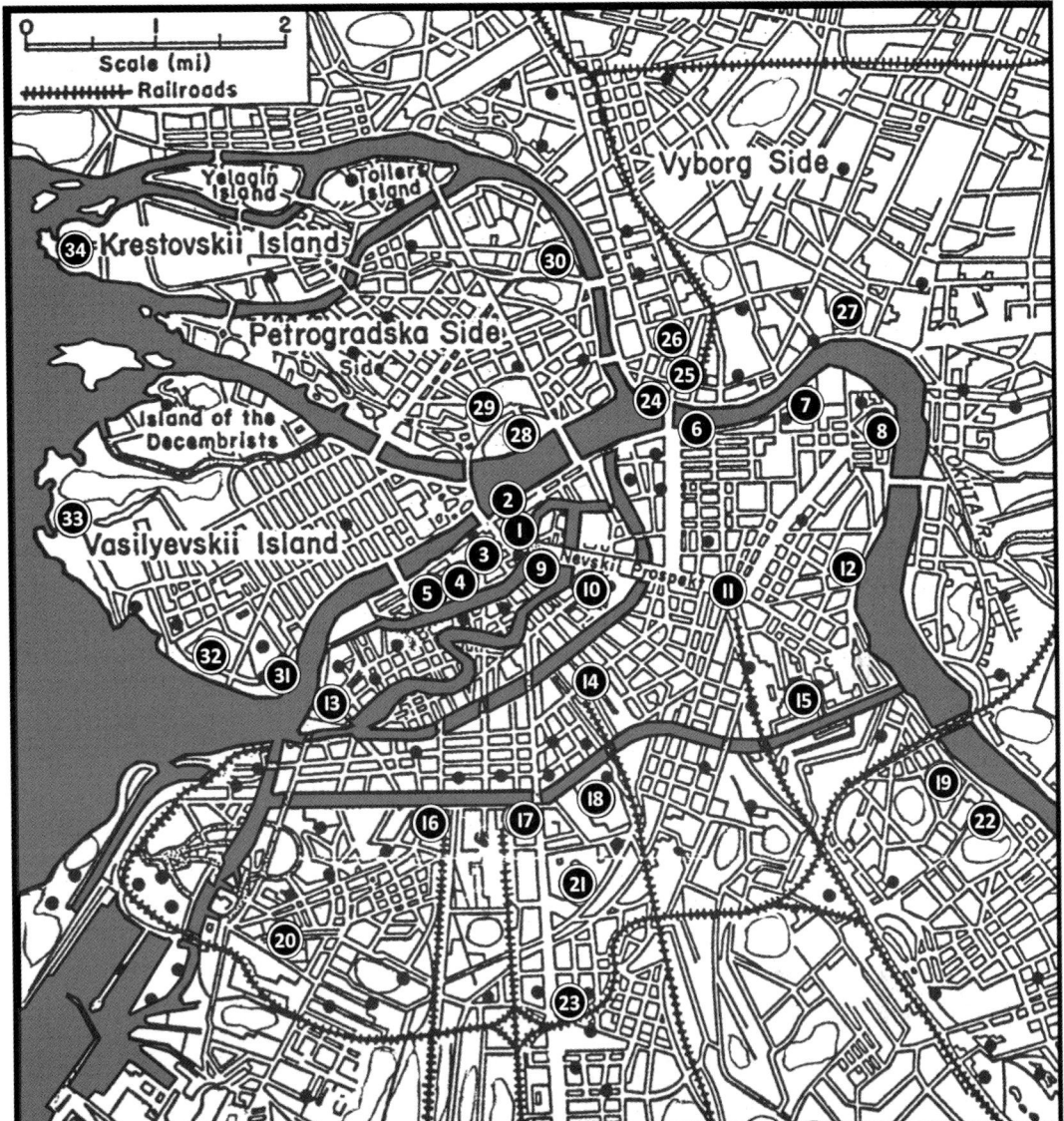

The Neva river and its tributaries divide Leningrad into a series of islands. This map shows the main locations: [1] Army HQ. [2] Hermitage. [3] Admiralty. [4] St Isaac's Cathedral. [5] Main Post Office. [6] NKVD HQ. [7] Main Water Works. [8] Smolny Institute. [9] Kazan Cathedral. [10] Gostiny Dvor. [11] Moscow Railway Station. [12] Electric Power Station. [13] Marti Shipyards. [14] Vitebsk Railway Station. [15] Electric Power Station. [16] Baltic Railway Station. [17] Warsaw Railway Station. [18] Main Gas Works and Electric Power Station. [19] Kirov Flourmill. [20] Kirov Works. [21] Badayev Food Warehouses. [22] Lenin Works. [23] Elektrosila Works. [24] Liteiny Bridge. [25] Finland Railway Station. [26] Military Medical Academy. [27] Stalin Works. [28] Peter and Paul Fortress. [29] Zoo. [30] Botanical Garden. [31] Baltic Shipyards. [32] Electric Power Station. [33] Army Food Storage. [34] Stadium. Black dots indicate areas of major damage from German air and artillery bombardment.

seemed far away. It was summertime and to most people in the city the only signs of the approaching war were a few high-flying aircraft and the occasional sound of distant artillery, which they could hear drawing nearer with each day as summer unfolded. It was apparent to all that, unless defences could be rapidly constructed and held, the Germans would soon be at the gates of the city.

Like all great cities, Leningrad was rich in statues and sculptures. To protect these priceless works of art against damage from shelling or bombing, they were either removed to safe storage or clad in a protective covering. Here a labour detail of men and women work to construct a blast protection around the equestrian statue of Peter the Great on Ploschad Dekabristov (Decembrists Square). St Isaac's Cathedral stands in the background. (Novosti)

The famous statue, better known as the Bronze Horseman, still stands on its huge 1,600-tonne pedestal rock.

The covered statue with anti-tank obstacles obstructing the Neva embankment road and Decembrists Square. The long façade in the background is the Admiralty building. (Novosti)

It was snow and mud rather than steel that hindered traffic in Vladimir's comparison.

Leningrad Prepares for Siege • **23**

Soldiers march past the Admiralty building. Standing on the Neva waterfront at the convergence of the city's three main avenues – Nevsky Prospect, Ghorokovaya Ulitsa and Voznezenskiy Prospect – and with its slender gold-sheathed spire rising high above its 407-metre-long façade, the building is still one of the main landmarks in Leningrad. (Novosti)

The small street along which the troops once marched is Admiralty Drive.

RENEWED GERMAN OFFENSIVE

ON 2ND JULY, Heeregruppe Nord started the second stage of its advance, when it struck out from its bridgeheads across the Dvina. The line of advance from that river to Leningrad was constricted by two big lakes – Lake Peipus along the old Estonian-Russian-border and Lake Ilmen further to the east – so the renewed offensive aimed to capture the 'land bridge' between these two water expanses. On 4th July, Panzergruppe 4 reached the Velikaya river that flows northward into Lake Peipus and which marked the pre-1939 border with Latvia. Three important towns lie on its banks: from north to south, Pskov, Ostrov and Opochka. Reinhardt's XXXXI Panzerkorps took

German infantry in the Luga area, photographed in July 1941. (SSETO)

Ostrov on the 4th, defeated a Soviet counter-attack on the 5th - destroying 140 tanks in the process. They then proceeded to capture Pskov on the 8th. Meanwhile, Manstein's LVI Panzerkorps took Opochka. Due to supply problems and the difficult, marshy terrain encountered beyond the river, the German advance from the Ostrov bridgehead slowed down, and Panzergruppe 4 was forced to divert Reinhardt's XXXXI Panzerkorps north-eastward, closer to the Baltic coast, to open up a new line of advance. On 14th July, having bypassed whatever Russian concentrations stood in their way, Reinhardt's panzer spearheads reached the Luga river, the last main obstacle before Leningrad only 60 miles from the city.

The river, which flows north-westward from Lake Ilmen to the Gulf of Finland, was also Leningrad's outermost defence line. Hastily constructed by the efforts of 300,000 mainly civilian workers in a two-week period, the Luga Line chiefly consisted of an anti-tank ditch, which stretched for 100 miles, reinforced sparsely with pillboxes, trenches and dragon's teeth anti-tank obstacles. The commander of the line was Major-General K. P. Pyadyshev. All he had to man his defences were six rifle divisions and a mountain brigade, all of low fighting value, plus stragglers and broken units from the earlier fighting. Any hope of holding the Luga Line lay with the Opolcheni, the volunteer militia units, three of which arrived from Leningrad to bolster the defence. The 1st Division of Volunteers had taken over an 18-mile front from Unomer to Kositskoye on 10th July; the 2nd Division arrived on 14th July and occupied positions at Ivanoskoye; the 3rd Division went into the line on the 15th.

The haste and carelessness with which the volunteer units had been organised resulted in a deadly toll once they were put into action. Many of the volunteers never even reached the fighting lines as they were overcome by age, illness and fatigue. One commander reported losing 200 out of his 1,000 men during a route march to the front. While unable to stop the enemy advance, the Opolcheni volunteers did succeed in buying time for the city, although at a terrible cost. Frequently they were thrown into battles when the front had already broken. By sheer weight of numbers and courage rather than by any military skills they held up the Germans, but their losses were enormous with some 100,000 casualties being incurred before the front was stabilised and the defence duties were taken over by regular formations.

General von Leeb's forces were worn out by the bloody fighting of the previous weeks, forcing him to give up his idea of a single concentrated lightning panzer strike towards Leningrad. He now planned a double envelopment of the city by his two panzer corps, with Reinhardt's XXXXI Panzerkorps on the left being supported on the flank by 18. Armee and Manstein's LVI Panzerkorps on the right receiving similar assistance from 16. Armee.

When the German attack on the Luga Line came on 8th August, the Russian soldiers fought bravely and tenaciously, but their lack of armour and artillery put them at an irrevocable disadvantage. By 11th August, the line had

A map from the *Manchester Guardian* of 9th September 1941, giving a clear idea of the key locations in the northern sector of the Russian front. The progress of the campaign was followed closely in the British press, the Soviets presenting that unusual commodity – an ally – on the European continent.

been breached in the Kingisepp sector on the German left flank. A surprise counter-attack by the Soviet 38th Army against the right flank of the 16. Armee gave only temporary respite. The LVI Panzerkorps made a rapid manoeuvre and was able to nip off the counter-attack before it could make headway.

By 12th August, the Germans were behind the Luga Line and advancing rapidly. The Soviet forces folded and were forced to withdraw in confusion. On 13th August, Manstein's LVI Panzerkorps captured the old city of Novgorod, thus severing the main Moscow to Leningrad highway.

On 21st August, the Leningrad administration issued a proclamation as follows:

> 'Comrade Leningraders! Dear Friends, our dearly beloved city is in imminent danger of attack, the Red Army is striving valiantly to defend the approaches to our city, but the enemy has not yet been crushed, his resources are not yet exhausted, he wants to destroy our homes, to drench our streets and squares with the blood of innocent victims, to outrage our peaceful population, to enslave the free sons of our Motherland. Never shall this be. The enemy is at the gates. Let us rise like one man in defence of our city, our homes, our families, honour and freedom.'

THE BALTIC FLEET WITHDRAWS TO LENINGRAD

WHILE HOEPNER'S PANZERGRUPPE 4 was sweeping northwards towards Leningrad, von Küchler's 18. Armee was steadily advancing along the Baltic coast towards the Gulf of Finland. German control of the Denmark Straits had effectively turned the Baltic Sea into a large German-controlled lake preventing Russian shipping from being able to access the world's oceans. This also prevented the Western Allies from sending any supply convoys to aid Russia. However, the Soviet Baltic Fleet still had considerable numbers of surface vessels and submarines in the Baltic, either at sea or in ports like Riga in Latvia and Tallinn in Estonia. As the German 18. Armee advanced into the Baltic countries, the fleet was successively withdrawn eastwards. To restrict their free movement in the Gulf, the German and Finnish navies began a considerable mine-laying exercise.

On 23rd June, 1941, a German mine seriously damaged the cruiser *Maxim Gorki* during its journey back to Leningrad. Under tow, the cruiser managed to continue into Kronstadt naval base where she was repaired enough to allow her to later take a vital part in the defence of Leningrad. Stationed near the grain terminal in the commercial port, her 180mm guns were a welcome addition to the firepower of the defenders.

The Soviet Navy and merchant fleet suffered gruesome losses when they evacuated the port of Tallinn. German forces first surrounded the city on 8th August and launched their final attack on it late on the 19th. However, no less than 170 naval and merchant ships with some 23,000 refugees and troops aboard were able to evacuate the harbour before the port fell on 28th August. The first convoy to sail was led by the cruiser Kirov and included 15 destroyers, four torpedo boats, six submarines, 28 minesweepers and 26 merchant ships. The second convoy consisted of minesweepers, guard ships, submarine chasers and 62 merchant ships. Attacked by German aircraft and torpedo boats, shelled by artillery from the nearby shore and crippled by the closely set minefields, the convoys suffered terrible losses. Of a total of 67 civilian vessels, 34 were lost. Of the 29 large transports, 25 were sunk, three were beached on Hogland Island and only one reached Leningrad. More than 10,000 lives were lost. Of over 100 Navy warships, 16 were sunk. Less than two-thirds of the vessels survived to reach Kronstadt.

LENINGRAD ISOLATED

MEANWHILE THE ADVANCE by Panzergruppe 4 continued. On 25th August, Reinhardt's XXXXI Panzerkorps on the left reached Krasnogvardeisk, only 30 miles from Leningrad. Instead of having it press on towards the city, von Leeb ordered the corps southwards to link up with Manstein's LVI Panzerkorps near Novgorod in order to encircle and destroy sizable Soviet forces that were still on the Luga or withdrawing from it. The junction between the two corps, achieved on 31st August, captured 20,000 prisoners.

At the same time, Heeresgruppe Nord had been reinforced by the arrival of the XXXIX Panzerkorps, comprised of 12. Panzer-Division with 18. and 20. Infanterie-Divisions (both motorised), under the command of General Rudolf Schmidt. It had been detached from Panzergruppe 3 of Heeresgruppe Mitte to accelerate the drive on Leningrad. Committed on the left wing of Busch's 16. Armee, its task was to move on Leningrad from the south-east.

Often captioned as being the Bronze Horseman, this boarded-in statue is in fact that of Lenin, which stands in front of the Finland Railway Station (out of frame to the right). Finland Station was where the revolutionary returned from 17 years in exile on 3rd April, 1917, to be received by a huge crowd of cheering Bolsheviks, and where he again arrived in October of that year to begin the Bolshevik coup (Novosti)

When a new station was built in the 1950s the Lenin statue was moved south, closer to the Neva. The building in the right background of the wartime picture has not survived.

When the Germans captured Schlüsselburg on 8th September 1941, they ignored the small fortress island of Oreshek, which lies only 500 metres across the water at the entrance to the Neva river from Lake Ladoga. However, unknown to the Germans, and apparently also to the withdrawing Russian main forces, a group of 12 Russian sailors from the Ladoga Fleet were still deep within the subterranean chambers busy packing supplies oblivious to what was happening outside. However, the sailors soon became aware of their perilous position when they saw German troops digging in on the Schlüsselburg waterfront and building what appeared to be pontoons suitable for a river crossing. Frantically searching through the cellars for some weapons with which they could defend themselves, the sailors found two old cannon, both without sights, and these were quickly positioned pointing towards the attackers and fired. However, the Germans did not react immediately. Either they must have assumed that the fortress was heavily defended or they may have decided that, as this outpost was now cut off from all overland communication, they could just sit back and wait for the effects of the siege to take hold. When the Leningrad Front command realised that the fortress was still occupied by their own troops, reinforcements consisting of one officer and thirteen sailors from the Ladoga Fleet were ferried across, together with seven 45mm cannon and six machine guns. Sniper posts were constructed in the walls and the increased rate of fire made the Germans fully aware that the island was occupied and presented a threat to them. Their response was to direct heavy artillery fire at the ten-foot-thick outer walls, and over the following months many thousands of tons of high explosive rained down on the defenders. By 7th November, the small force was still in position and felt confident enough to raise the Red Flag over the fortress. It promptly drew fire but, although it was shot down six times during the course of the siege, it was still flying fourteen months later when the Red Army began its effort to relieve the encirclement in January 1943. The Germans carried out several forays against the fortress, but it was held by the Soviets throughout the siege, forming a lynchpin in the defence of the Ladoga Lake supply route.

The battle to encircle Leningrad was now entering its final stage. On 25th August, the two motorised divisions of Schmidt's XXXIX Panzerkorps captured Chudovo, on the main Moscow to Leningrad railway line. Then, on 29th August, the same two divisions took the town of Mga, an important railway centre 25 miles south-east of Leningrad. The loss of Mga was a serious blow to Leningrad because through it passed the Leningrad to Tikhvin railway line, the last remaining rail connection between the city and the Russian hinterland. All that remained now to bring supplies into

Today the fortress is being restored but part of the ruins have been preserved as a memorial to its heroic defenders.
(R. Hogg)

the city was the narrow land corridor, just seven miles wide, between Mga and the southern shores of Lake Ladoga.

On 6th September, Führer Directive No. 35 ordered Heeresgruppe Nord to transfer Panzergruppe 4 to Heeresgruppe Mitte in order to accelerate the latter's drive on Moscow. The order was to go into effect on 15th September, so von Leeb knew he would soon lose most of his armour. Nevertheless, he launched his drive into the Russian lines hoping to put a tight ring around Leningrad before the departure of the panzers. By now, faced with ever more tenacious Russian defence, the German advance had slowed to a crawl.

East of Leningrad, the XXXIX Panzerkorps closed the narrow land corridor remaining between Mga and Lake Ladoga. On 8th September, its 20. Infanterie-Division (mot.) scored a major success when, after a fierce battle, it captured the town of Schlüsselburg (Shlissel'burg), on the south-west corner of Lake Ladoga, 22 miles east of Leningrad, thus cutting the city's last overland communication links with the rest of Russia. Leningrad was now completely isolated. The only way left to bring in any supplies was by air or by ship across the waters of Lake Ladoga.

South-west of Leningrad the XXXXI Panzerkorps and XXXVIII Armeekorps attacked northwards to reach the coast of the Gulf of Finland. On 10th September, the 1. and 6. Panzer-Division occupied Krasnoye Selo, just seven-and-a-half miles south-west of Leningrad. On the 11th, the 1. Panzer-Division secured a foothold on the Duderhof heights, which gave the Germans a commanding view across the whole city.

Leningrad Isolated • 31

A column of troops marches past the protected statue of Tsar Nicholas I on Isaakievskaya Ploschad (St Isaac's Square). This picture was taken from a first-floor window of the Astoria Hotel, in the north-east corner of the square. (Novosti)

On 16th September, the 1. Panzer-Division, supported by 58. and 254. Infanterie-Divisions, slashed through the Russian lines and reached the coast of the Gulf of Finland near Strelna, and in so doing cut off the Soviet 8th Army from the other armies defending the Leningrad perimeter. Thus the Oranienbaum enclave came into being. Some ten miles deep and 20 miles wide, it stretched from the Gulf of Finland in the west to Peterhof in the east. Strongly encircled by German forces, this outpost would hold out valiantly against all odds throughout the entire blockade. Maintained across the ice from Kronstadt in winter and directly across the Gulf of Finland in warmer weather, it would form a constant thorn in the side of the besiegers. Attacking forays would be constantly made from the enclave.

On 18th September, the 1. Panzer-Division, in a final effort, broke through to reach Pulkovo crossroads and Aleksandrovka, the terminus of the Leningrad south-west tram line, just seven miles from the heart of the city. The Soviets, employing tanks straight from the Kolpino tank factory assembly line, tenaciously held on to the Pulkovo Heights and the German advance ground to a halt on its southern slopes.

As the fighting subsided in mid-September, four Soviet armies ended up trapped inside the Leningrad perimeter: the 23rd, 42nd and 55th Armies and the Neva Operational Group, totalling some 20 divisions. Also bottled up in the waters around Kronstadt was the Baltic Fleet. Despite

Unable to get access to the hotel room, Vladimir took his comparison from ground level on Bolshaya Morskaya.

its losses, the fleet at the beginning of the siege could still muster two battleships, two cruisers, 13 destroyers, 12 gunboats, 42 submarines, six coastal defence ships, nine armed cutters, 68 trawlers and minelayers, 38 torpedo boats and 134 miscellaneous craft. In addition, by 20th August, the Soviet Navy had put into action 170 shore batteries, including 48 railway guns, and formed six batteries around 13 large guns removed from the naval artillery proving ground. The combined firepower of the Navy warships and shore batteries represented a considerable artillery asset. This could, and did, provide devastating fire to assist the Soviet ground forces in their initial defence of the city and in the later break-out battles of 1943 and 1944.

The largest calibre guns were the 406mm static cannons with a range of 28 miles firing shells weighing approximately 2,440 pounds (1,108 kilograms). The 356mm guns were railway-mounted and fired shells weighing 1,649 pounds (748 kilos) to a range of 19 miles. The 305mm guns of the battleship Marat fired shells of 1,038 pounds (471 kilos) to a distance of 18 miles. However, the amount of ammunition available for these big guns was limited and most firing during the blockade was done by the medium calibre guns, which had ranges from 15 to 23 miles.

The naval batteries were integrated into the city's defence system that divided the force into three groups. The first was known as the Neva Group and consisted of the smaller craft such as gunboats, the smaller destroyers and minesweepers. These were positioned in the Neva river east of the

The guns of a naval vessel being deployed to supplement the city's air defences. The vessel is moored on the Neva River close to the Trinity bridge. In the background the spire of the Peter and Paul Cathedral can just be seen through the haze. (SSETO)

city, from Smolny to the Izhorsk region. The second detachment was known as the Leningrad Group and consisted of the cruiser Petropavlovsk, positioned at the coal wharfs, the cruiser Maxim Gorki stationed at the grain elevator and some smaller warships positioned around the commercial docks. The third and most powerful group was positioned in the Kronstadt/Oranienbaum anchorage area. This included the battleships Marat and October Revolution, the cruiser Kirov and several minelayers and patrol boats. During September 1941 this group alone laid down 358 barrages delivering 9,368 shells.

In the early stages of the blockade, Kronstadt and the ships of the fleet were very poorly protected from air attacks and Kronstadt's position grew even more difficult when German land batteries were brought into position to shell the fortress and shipping. The German gunners soon found the range of the ships in the seaway and on 16th September, the first 150mm shells hit the dreadnought Marat and the cruiser Petropavlovsk. On 18th September, the German batteries concentrated on the Petropavlovsk with some fire being directed at the Maxim Gorki. The Petropavlovsk was hit a total of eight times and eventually settled on the bottom. During a Luftwaffe attack on the ships on 21st September, the battleship October Revolution was hit. A fire broke out, but control and power were maintained and the ship was quickly taken in tow by a tug and moved into Kronstadt dockyard for repair.

On 23rd September, the Luftwaffe attacked the Marat when it was anchored in shallow waters just outside Kronstadt harbour. One bomb hit the foredeck, setting off an enormous explosion which caused the complete forward section of the ship to break off and the forward 'A' gun turret, with its three 305mm guns, to completely disappear under water. Hundreds of sailors were thrown into the water by the explosions and some 200 men, including the captain, Captain Ivanov, were killed or wounded. The main body of the ship settled down on an even keel. However, within a few days, and with the ingenuity and resourcefulness of the Russian crew, the three remaining gun turrets, each with three 305mm guns, were again fully operational.

Where they could not be used offensively, the guns of a number of ships were demounted and put into service as land batteries. Guns from the cruiser Aurora (which had fired blanks on the Winter Palace in November of 1917 to frighten the Kerensky Government ministers into surrendering to Lenin's Bolsheviks) were placed on the Pulkovo Heights south of the city. Armament factories in Leningrad engaged in round-the-clock work to manufacture and assemble mountings for Navy gun barrels.

The catastrophic events of early September led to a change of command on the Soviet side. Marshal Kliment E. Voroshilov, who had taken over from Popov as the commander of the Leningrad Front on 13th July, had not dared to report the loss of Mga and Schlüsselburg to Stalin. When the dictator did find out, he relieved Voroshilov of his command on 11th September, calling on Marshal Georgi K. Zhukov to replace him. Just two months earlier, Stalin had dismissed Zhukov as Chief of the General Staff but the latter had regained new credit when, appointed to command the Central Front, at which time he had successfully delayed the advance of Heeregruppe Mitte at Yelnya. Zhukov flew to Leningrad on the 13th and immediately began reorganising the front, relieving weak commanders and issuing uncompromising orders.

It appeared that he had worked a miracle when the situation stabilised and the enemy pressure subsided. This was however not so much Zhukov's achievement, but more a direct result of Hitler's orders to von Leeb to surround the city, but not to enter it, and to transfer Panzergruppe 4 from the Leningrad front south to Moscow.

Zhukov was in command of the Leningrad Front for just four weeks. On 7th October, faced with the imminent attack on Moscow, Stalin ordered him back to the capital and gave him command of the forces there. In due course Lieutenant-General M. S. Khozin took over as commander of the Leningrad Front.

THE FINNS CLOSE THE RING FROM THE NORTH

AT THE SAME time as German forces were sealing off Leningrad from the south, the city was also being isolated from the north. This came about as a result of the Soviet Union's aggressive policy towards Finland during the pre-war years. Russia demanded a realignment of the Russian-Finnish border in Karelia, the territory immediately to the north of Leningrad, plus the strategically important island port of Hanko at the head of the Gulf of Finland. Russia had no reason to fear Finland, a relatively small country, but the developing political situation in Europe had created a new awareness to the possibility of an invasion taking place through Finland, and Russia considered that it needed the additional territories as a buffer for its defence. Negotiations between the two governments soon broke down and on 30th November, 1939, Soviet forces attacked Finland, starting what became known as the Winter War. Heavy ground attacks were launched against the Mannerheim Line, the Finnish defence line across the Karelian Isthmus north of Leningrad, with other attacks being launched north of Lake Ladoga, in central Finland, and in the far north.

Finish troops were able to push back the Russian Army all the way to the 1939 border, during the 'Continuation War'. Finnish troops wear a variety of headgear including, in the case of the two nearest soldiers, the German M16 helmet of First World War vintage. (SSETO)

Many believed that the vastly outnumbered Finnish forces would be rapidly defeated but this was not the case. The Finnish Army was inadequately equipped, but they were well trained in winter warfare and strongly motivated to defend their home country. Their ski troops were masters at the art of rapid attack and withdrawal. The Red Army troops, surprisingly unprepared for winter fighting and unfamiliar with the type of terrain encountered, suffered a series of costly defeats. Reassessing their strategy, the Soviets abandoned their effort to drive through the snowbound northern wildernesses and subsequent attacks on the Mannerheim Line were better coordinated with a massive superiority in artillery, aircraft and men. After two months of strenuous effort, a breakthrough was achieved. On 11th March, 1940, Russian troops occupied Viipuri (now Vyborg) and the next day the Finnish Government surrendered. The Moscow peace treaty signed on 12th March gave the Soviet Union all the border modifications and the naval base at Hanko they had originally demanded.

Fifteen months later, the German invasion of Russia in June 1941 gave Finland the opportunity to restore the old situation. Now an ally of Germany, they attacked on 31st July, starting what became known as the 'Continuation War'. Advancing rapidly

Field Marshal Carl Gustav von Mannerheim, Commander-in-Chief of the Finish Army. (SSETO)

against the Soviet 23rd Army down both sides of Lake Ladoga, by 7th September the Finnish forces had regained all their old border positions. Strong defensive positions were then established among the forests and lakes along the Mannerheim Line, right across the Karelian Isthmus, effectively sealing off Leningrad from the north. On the eastern side of Lake Ladoga, the Finns had reached the line of the Svir river, just a short distance across the old frontier. However, despite repeated German requests, the Finns were reluctant to continue further into Russian territory to effect a link-up with the German forces approaching from the south. The Finnish leader, Field Marshal Carl Gustav von Mannerheim, had a clear political reason for this: the Finns had no desire to pursue occupation of a neighbouring country that they would no doubt have to live alongside of in the future.

The Finns close the ring from the North

BEGINNING OF THE SIEGE

BY AUGUST, HITLER had changed his plans towards Leningrad. He had decided to lay siege to the city rather than capture it. His new orders told von Leeb not to enter the city but to go around it and link up with the Finns. Once cut off from all supplies, the city was to be bombed and shelled into

German bombing raids on the city started on 6th September 1941 and remained a continuous threat throughout the siege. That month alone, the Luftwaffe carried out eleven daylight attacks and twelve night-time raids, with an estimated 480 aircraft out of the total force of 2,712 bombers penetrating the city defences. Boris Kudoyarov photographed the momentary panic on Nevsky Prospect as civilians, and a troop of soldiers on horseback, rush to find shelter during an air raid alarm. (Novosti)

38 • THE SEIGE OF LENINGRAD – THEN AND NOW

submission during the winter months. The population and military garrison were to be starved and frozen to death. It would save the Germans the heavy losses involved in a frontal attack on the city and spare them the trouble of having to feed three million extra mouths. Von Leeb was to refuse any Soviet offer to surrender.

With the departure of Panzergruppe 4 in mid-September, it remained for the 18. Armee to carry out this directive. German offensive action moved eastwards, to the Volkhov and Tikhvin area, where Schmidt's XXXIX Armeekorps fought to achieve the desired link-up with the Finns on the Svir. Meanwhile the 18. Armee's infantry divisions laid an iron ring around Leningrad, with the XXVI and L Armeekorps containing the

Nevsky Prospect is St Petersburg's most important and grandiose avenue, the city's equivalent of the Champs Elysées in Paris, or Berlin's Unter den Linden. Three miles long, it runs in a straight line from the Admiralty building on the Neva, south-west to the Alexander Nevsky Monastery beyond the Fontanka river. The picture was taken at the intersection with Malaya Sadovaya Street. The trees on the right mark Ploschad Ostrovskovo (Ostrovsky Square), but known to the locals as 'Katya's Garden' after the statue of Catherine the Great that stands in the park.

Beginning of the Seige • 39

Oranienbaum bridgehead and holding the line south of the city, with the XXVIII Armeekorps occupying the vital Schlüsselburg salient. Both sides began digging in, building an ever-more elaborate system of trenches, dugouts, bunkers and permanent artillery positions. Static warfare set in, reminiscent of the trench warfare of the First World War. For the next two and a half years, ground fighting in much of this sector would be limited to patrolling and small-scale actions.

Leningrad at the start of the siege had an estimated civilian population of 2,544,000, including 400,000 children. Another 343,000 people (including refugees from other cities) were estimated to be living outside of the city, but within the blockade perimeter. In addition, there were the military forces defending the city including the naval forces in Kronstadt and the troops entrapped in the Oranienbaum enclave, estimated at 500,000. The total number of people within the blockade who would require feeding was therefore close to 3,400,000.

The city was totally unprepared for a winter siege. On 1st July, rationing had been introduced in all big cities of the Soviet Union but since then there had been no change in allowance, with the rations being close to normal consumption. Workers still received 800 grams of bread a day and 2,200 grams of meat per month, together with an ample allowance of wheat, sugar and fat. Dependents and children received 400 grams of bread. Rationing was not very strict either and there were many exceptions. Even commercial restaurants were still allowed to sell food outside the system.

It was only at the end of August that the city authorities first began to worry about the diminishing food supplies in the city. Taking stock of reserves on hand, they discovered that on the basis of the current allowance, they was only enough to last one month. On 29th August – the day the Germans took Mga, severing the last rail connection with the rest of Russia – the Leningrad authorities sent an urgent telegram to Moscow asking for emergency food shipments to be sent by train to the eastern shore of Lake Ladoga, which they hoped could then be transported by boat across the lake and up the Neva river to the city. In line with these arrangements the city rations were cut on 2nd September. The daily bread allowance was reduced to 600 grams for workers, 400 grams for office workers, and 300 grams for dependents and children under 12. Meat and cereals were cut to 1,400 grams a month, fats to 250 grams, and sweets to 2,500 grams.

On 4th September, the first German artillery shell fell on the city. It was the start of a long campaign of regular shelling, which would harass the city population for many months to come and would cost thousands of lives. In September alone there would be 200 artillery barrages. By the end of 1941 a total of 30,154 shells would have landed in the city.

The first German air raid on the city was launched on 6th September. A further twenty-three raids rained destruction on the city that month. On the 8th, the Luftwaffe's Ju 88 bombers returned in force and disaster struck for Leningrad when German bombs hit the Badayev district in the

Anti-aircraft guns in action against German aircraft, photographed by Boris Kudoyarov. These guns are dug in on Ploschad Dekabristov (Decembrists Square), just south of the equestrian statue of Peter the Great. St Isaac's Cathedral looms against the evening sky in the background. During the Luftwaffe's intensive bombing campaign of September 1941 the city's anti-aircraft guns, together with the aircraft of the VII Fighter Aviation Corps, claimed to have shot down 272 enemy aircraft. (Novosti)

A perfect comparison by Vladimir Skvortsov, taken looking south-east across Ploschad Dekabristov.

Beginning of the Seige • 41

Anti-aircraft position on the Strelka, the spit of Vasilyevsky Island that lies just north of the city centre across the Neva river. Anti-aircraft defence of the city was the responsibility of the II Air Defence Corps which, at the beginning of the war, comprised the 115th, 169th, 189th, 192nd, 194th and 351st Anti-Aircraft Artillery Regiments and numbered 950 AA guns, 230 machine guns, 300 searchlights, 360 barrage balloons, 302 forward early-warning observation posts and eight radio-location sites. Later the city's anti-aircraft capability was reinforced by the anti-aircraft units of the 23rd, 42nd and 55th Armies trapped within the blockade perimeter, aided by the guns of the Baltic Fleet. (Novosti)

south of the city, where much of the city's food reserves was stored in central warehouses. The flames spread from one wooden warehouse to another, soon engulfing the whole area in an inferno of fire which attracted even more bombers. All 168 of the city's fire-brigade crews were sent to Badayev to fight the conflagration but to no avail. The results were catastrophic. An estimated 3,000 tons of flour were lost. All of the city's sugar reserves, 2500 tons in all, melted and streamed down in the warehouse cellars where it hardened into a kind of black caramelised concrete.

The Germans cut the city's last overland supply line on 8th September, the same day on which they captured Schlüsselburg. That same fateful day, Dmitri V. Pavlov, a young, able and energetic executive of the Defence Commissariat's Main Administration of Food Supplies, arrived in Leningrad from Moscow vested with power to handle all food questions in Leningrad, both for the civilians and the military. In two days, he made a thorough inventory of what food reserves were still on hand in the city after the Badayev disaster. Based on the current ration allowances, the totals were: grain, flour and hardtack for 35 days; cereals and macaroni for 30 days; meat

The same view today. On the left stands one of the famous twin Rostral Columns, former 19th-century lighthouses copied from the Imperial Roman custom of erecting columns decorated with the sawn-off prows, or rostrae, of captured Carthaginian galleys. The 19th-century warehouse building on the right is today the Zoological Museum. Hidden behind the Rostral Column lies Dvortsovy Most (Palace Bridge). The dome of St Isaac's Cathedral can be seen across the river.

and meat products including live cattle for 33 days; fat for 45 days; sugar and confectionary for 60 days.

Pavlov took immediate measures. Realising the danger of reliance on central supply depots, he ordered the flour and grain supplies divided over various distribution points around the city. He stopped the sale of all food without ration coupons, closed down commercial restaurants, and forbade any slaughter of cattle without permission. On 10th September, the bread allowance for industrial workers was decreased again, from 600 to 500 grams per day.

Looking for means to increase the resources available, Pavlov realised that there were still crops in the fields, gardens and abandoned farms around the city. Harvesting of potatoes and vegetables was given a high priority and, although the suburban regions were often under German fire, a total of 2,352 tons were collected by 20th September, and a further 7,300 tons were brought in before the ground froze.

Wanting to clean up the ration-card system, on 10th October Pavlov decreed that all cards needed to be re-registered between 12th and 18th October. He enlisted a force of 3,000 Party workers to carry out a thorough

Beginning of the Seige • 43

Heavy anti-aircraft guns dug in on Marsovo Pole (Field of Mars), Leningrad's largest square. In an effort to improve command efficiency, in November 1941 the II Air Defence Corps was converted into the Leningrad Corps Air Defence Region, directly subordinate to the Leningrad Front commander. Anti-aircraft regiments established well-coordinated fire zones on the outskirts and in the city itself, concentrating mainly along the western and south-western approaches to the city. The growing strength and flexibility of Leningrad's AA defences caused the German air bombardment to decrease sharply between January and March 1942, dwindling to individual aircraft in April and ceasing altogether from May to October. (Novosti)

Looking north across the Field of Mars today. The buildings in the background are (L-R) the North-West Polytechnic University (formerly the service wing of the Marble Palace); the Troitskiy Most (Trinity Bridge) across the Neva river; the Academy of Culture (the former Saltykov Palace); and the Betskov House.

Worse than the bombing was the shelling, which began on 4th September. German artillery pounded Leningrad 272 times during the last four months of 1941, firing 5,364 rounds in September, 7,590 in October, 11,230 in November, and 5,970 in December. On some days, shells would fall uninterrupted for more than 18 hours. Here, as smoke from a shell explosion lingers between the buildings, three women run for cover at Anichkov Most, the bridge that crosses the Fontanka river on Nevsky Prospect. Note the boy across the street watching the scene, seemingly oblivious to the danger. (Novosti)

To save them from harm, the famous bronze horse sculptures decorating the four corners of the bridge were removed from their pedestals and buried in the grounds of the nearby Anichkov Palace. Today, the sculptures are back in place.

Beginning of the Seige • 45

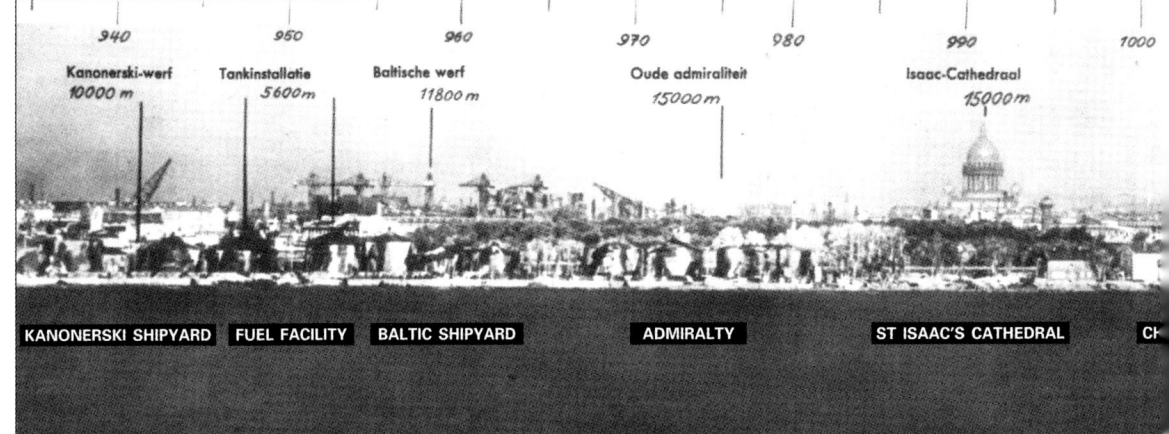

Just how close the Germans were to the city is illustrated by this panorama of Leningrad's skyline, shot with a telephoto lens from the Pulkovo Heights for artillery registration purposes. Important landmarks and military targets are indicated together with their range. This picture appeared in the Dutch-language edition of the German propaganda magazine Signal of May 1942. The German 18. Armee had concentrated its siege artillery in two main groups, one north of Krasnoye Selo and the other north of Mga. The former group comprised over 250 guns and included the heavy 28cm K5 railway guns of Eisenbahn-Artillerie-Abteilung 679 and from August 1942 the super-heavy siege mortars Dora (80cm) and Karl (60cm).

Boris Kudoyarov pictured a shell exploding on Nevsky Prospect. One of the best-known photographs to come out of the Leningrad blockade, this is in fact a montage of two different shots. The corpses on the right, although certainly real, are clearly out of scale with the civilians seen on the pavement on the left. They are, in fact, taken from the photograph on page 48, flipped horizontally. (Novosti)

1010	1020	1030	1040	1050	1060	1070	

Martiwerf 12100m · Schoorsteen van de Martiwerf 12100m · Pakhuis ten westen van de graanhaven 8000m · Gieterij en constructiewerkplaats 12100m · Smolny-klooster 19600m

MARTI SHIPYARD · **WAREHOUSE OF GRAIN TERMINAL** · **CHIMNEY OF MARTI SHIPYARD** · **FOUNDRY AND ENGINEERING WORKS** · **SMOLNY CONVENT**

check on all cards in the city. As expected they found many irregularities: forged cards, cards printed without official permission, people holding more than one card, or cards that were not rightfully possessed by the holder. All offenders were severely punished. The clean-up took some 280,000 irregular cards out of circulation.

But with the ever-diminishing stocks, rations continued to sink. As of 1st October, soldiers at the front received 800 grams of bread per day, plus

Notwithstanding the efforts of the photographic artist, the original photo was taken on Nevsky Prospect at the crossroads with Liteiny Prospect. The view is westward.

Beginning of the Seige • 47

A Red Army soldier stops to look at five victims of an artillery barrage lying on the corner of Nevsky and Ligovsky Prospects. (Novosti)

This picture was taken just two blocks further to the west from where that on page 46 was taken. Today the spot is just a quiet corner on Nevsky Prospect.

Death stalks the streets of Leningrad. These victims of German shelling lie on Ligovsky Prospect. Having fired over 30,000 shells into the city in the last four months of 1941, the guns fired another 21,000 shells into the city in 1942. A further 15,000 shells struck the city in the first half of 1943, but thereafter the artillery bombardment diminished, some 5,500 shells coming down in the second half of that year. (Novosti)

hot soup and stew (or to put it in ingredients: 150 grams of meat, 80 grams of fish, 140 grams of cereal, 500 grams of potatoes and vegetable, 50 grams of fat and 35 of sugar); industrial workers received half as much bread – 400 grams per day – and only 1,500 grams of meat per month; all other adults and children received only 200 grams of bread (two slices) per day and just 400 grams of meat per month, and about half the fat, cereals and sugar received by the workers.

On 9th November, the military rations were cut. Front-line troops now received 600 grams of bread

Ligovsky Prospect today, looking south.

Beginning of the Seige • 49

Generals Ritter von Leeb and Georg von Küchler scan the outskirts of the Leningrad perimeter, believed to be on the Duderhof heights, southwest of the city. The photograph was taken on 11th October 1941. SSETO

and 125 of meat; rear echelons got 400 grams of bread and 50 of meat. On 13th November, civilian rations were further reduced too, this time to 300 grams of bread (three slices) per day for factory workers and 150 grams for everyone else.

On 20th November, daily rations reached what would be their all-time low: 500 grams of bread for front-line troops, 300 for rear units, 250 for factory workers and a mere 125 grams for all the others. To make matters worse, the quality of the bread was by now steadily getting poorer due to the use of ingredients to replace flour – 'edible' cellulose, pine and fir bark, sawdust.

Troops performing the horrible job of removing victims after an artillery raid on Ploschad Vosstania (Insurrection Square). Between September 1941 and the end of 1943, a total of 5,723 civilians were killed and another 20,507 wounded by enemy shelling and bombing.

Few of today's passers-by will be aware of the bloody scenes witnessed by this corner of Leningrad eighty-three years ago. The building in the background is Moscow Railway Station.

With no coal or electricity, wood became the only source of fuel, but even this was terribly scarce. Kudoyarov photographed a firewood collecting point behind Kazan Cathedral, the grand church on the south side of Nevsky Prospect. (Novosti)

WINTER 1941–42

WINTER COLD STRUCK the city population earlier than hunger. By the end of September, all coal and fuel reserves for domestic use had been spent. To get replacement fuel, the city authorities organised firewood to be cut from the forests north of the city. Woodcutting teams of women and teenagers worked in freezing cold felling trees. Despite their heroic efforts, fuel remained scarce. By mid-October power production had fallen to one-third of its pre-war level.

By December, central heating in offices, flats and factories was switched off, and people were forced to live and work dressed in thick overcoats,

During the Communist era, Kazan Cathedral housed the infamous Museum of Atheism. Renamed the Museum of Religion during perestroika, it was moved out in 1999, and Kazan is now back in use as a place of worship.

The 'starvation winter' of 1941-42. Thickly dressed against the freezing cold, citizens queue up for water at a broken main on Nevsky Prospect. The long building on the left is Gostiny Dvor, Leningrad's largest shopping bazaar. A few weeks earlier, on 19th September 1941, a bomb had struck the building killing 98 and wounding another 148. (Novosti)

wearing fur hats and gloves. Houses ruined by shelling or bombardment were scavenged for anything that could burn. Small makeshift stoves – the burzhuiki – were constructed in workshops to provide some basic element of warmth for cooking and comfort and they were kept going using books, letters, furniture and just anything that would burn. They also caused hundreds of fires.

By mid-December, all but one of the city's power works had closed down for lack of coal. With water-pumping stations out of action and temperatures reaching minus 40°C, water mains froze. The water supply was shut down. Laundries and public baths ceased to operate. People were forced to get water from the Neva, hacking a hole in the ice and hauling up the muddy water with buckets.

The first cases of death from starvation occurred in October. At first, there were just a few cases every day but the number increased rapidly. The city hospitals quickly filled up with victims of the famine. Soon there were whole wards full of emaciated and dying people, treated by overworked staff who themselves were tottering on their legs from hunger and weakness. Official figures recorded 11,000 deaths in November, and 53,000 in December. On Christmas Day alone, 3,700 people died – the highest number of deaths on a single day.

Looking west down Nevsky Prospect today. The ornamental tower in the far background, known as the Ferrari Tower, marks the building of the former city Duma, the seat of the pre-revolutionary municipal government.

On 9th December, public transport in the city ceased due to lack of fuel. Many people, forced to walk to their jobs or duties, just did not have sufficient strength to complete their journeys and collapsed on the streets. Passers-by were not always inclined to assist those who fell, as they themselves were too weak to do anything positive. Snow soon drifted over the bodies of those who had fallen and their whereabouts would often not be known until the spring thaw. People who died in their homes had often to lie where they fell until sufficient friends and relatives could be collected to make a joint effort to move the bodies. Frequently notification of the death to the authorities was delayed so that the survivors might benefit from the deceased's ration card for a while. With no wood available for coffins, mass graves were opened in cemeteries and on bombed-out sites using military explosives.

The continual bombing and shelling caused considerable damage to the city's water and sewage systems and, as repairs were almost impossible to make, some streets had vast areas of sewage and refuse in them. This made them ideal breeding grounds for disease and infection, a situation worsened by the accumulation of dead bodies in the streets and the many open burial pits. Fortunately, the sub-zero temperatures, together with the actions taken by the authorities, prevented the occurrence of any serious epidemics during the blockade. One typhus outbreak was reported in a children's

This picture, (above left), which perhaps more than any other has come to symbolise the ordeal of the people of Leningrad, was taken by Mikhail Trakhman. Two heavily-clad women dragging a shrouded corpse down Nevsky Prospect on their way to the mortuary. However, few people will know that Trakhman took several shots of the same scene (above and opposite). Books on the Leningrad siege usually publish only one of them and, because the successive images differ so very little, most people will have assumed they were looking at the same picture. Trakhman, a special correspondent/photographer for the Soviet news agency TASS, who spent some time in the besieged city, must have been so struck by the dramatic impact of the scene that he wanted to make sure he achieved a good image. Although intruding into what was essentially a private family tragedy, he probably felt less inhibited because he was photographing the scene from the rear. (Novosti)

hospital in February 1942 but prompt isolation contained the disease.

For a while, rats, driven from the granaries and warehouses by lack of food, infested the open streets but most of them were soon caught and eaten as were any cats, dogs and birds that could be found. The need for food overtook any qualms or squeamishness. Horses and ponies, already desperately thin due to lack of fodder, that fell in the streets were cut up on the spot for food. People cooked leather belts and briefcases to extract a substance referred to as 'pork jelly'.

Scavenging parties scoured the city leaving no place unexamined in the search for food. Flour sacks were beaten and the flour dust saved. Floor sweepings from a tannery were also saved and mixed with sawdust to make a type of cake. A huge find of cellulose intended as ship's boiler fuel, but now unused, was processed to add to bread which was found to be edible although its nutritional value was negligible. Eight thousand tons of malt were also found in an abandoned brewery and put to good use.

With typical Russian resourcefulness, even a part of the foodstuffs lost in the disastrous fire of the Badayev warehouses was recovered. Some 700

Nevsky Prospect looking east. Just visible on the right is a corner of the Leningrad Public Library, today the Russian National Library.

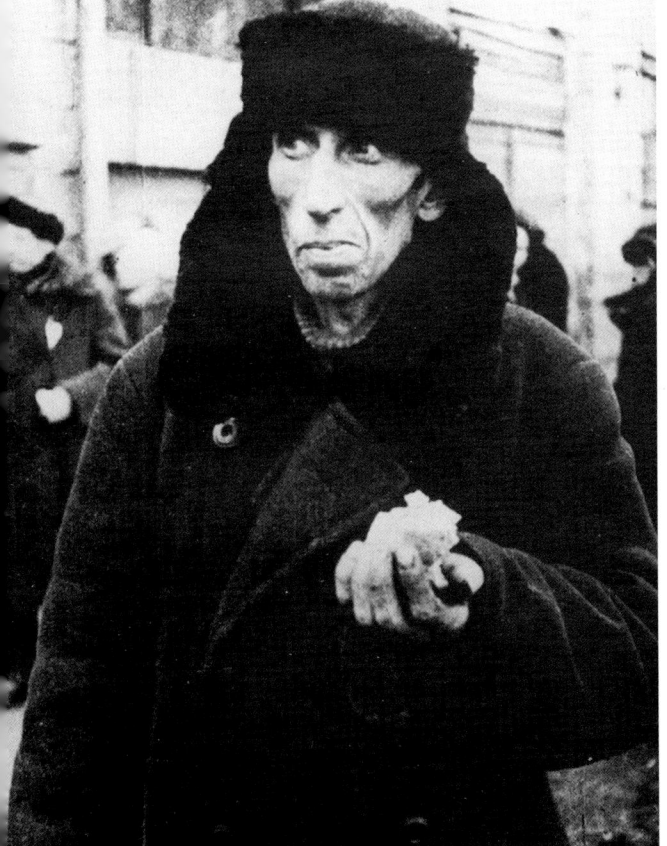

The effects of starvation are clearly visible in the features of this man holding his daily bread ration.

Yet scenes like that pictured by Trakhman were everyday sights in besieged Leningrad. At a time when death was more common than a slice of bread, passers-by pay little attention as a woman pulls a dead body – perhaps a close relative – on a sled across Lieutenant Shmidt Bridge. This bridge across the Neva connects the city centre with Vasilyevsky Island to the north. (It honours Lieutenant Piotr Schmidt who led a mutiny aboard the cruiser *Ochakov* during the 1905 revolution.)

of the 2,500 tons of the blackened, dirty and scorched sugar were reclaimed and processed to make a type of 'candy'. It tasted like rubber and had to be chewed like gum, but it did have some nutritional value. A quantity of the flour lost in the fire was also recovered and used.

The city's scientific community made every effort to find substitute foods from the materials available. Every avenue was examined. Books were stripped of their covers and the glue used in the bindings was melted down as an ingredient in soup; hair oil was used as fat; the intestines of rats and cats were rendered down and used to make a glutinous paste that was eaten spread on bread, when it was available. Wallpaper was removed from apartment walls and boiled to extract the flour paste glue commonly used at that time. A find of 2,000 tons of sheep gut in a warehouse, destined for musical instrument strings, was rapidly tuned into sausages by the addition of flax seeds and machine oil.

A scientific team headed by V. I. Sharkov of the Wood Products Institute succeeded in making tons of paste from the stewed branches of young trees mixed with peat and salt. This concoction was used to feed horses at the front. The oats that were normally given to the horses was mixed with malt and cocoa and used to make a form of bread for distribution to the city population. Sharkov's team also worked out a formula for edible cellulose

Looking west from the bridge today, the tall dome in the background is that of the Kiev Cave Monastery (Kievopecherskaya Lavra) Mission.

made from pine sawdust. It was added to the bread and nearly 16,000 tons were consumed during the blockade. Many of the alternative foods gave no, or very little, nourishment but at least gave those who ate them a brief relief from the gnawing hunger.

Many of the inhabitants suffered from scurvy due to the prolonged restricted diet. A scientist, Professor A. D. Bezzubov, discovered a process to extract vitamin C from pine needles. Komsomol youths collected 40 truckloads of pine needles from the forests to the north of the city, and over 16 million doses of this 'medicine' were produced in 1942 and distributed throughout the city.

As always under conditions of siege and famine, there were egoists and profiteers: people engaging in hoarding and black-market activities; persons stealing other people's ration cards or robbing them of food, fuel or clothes; bakers fiddling with the prescribed measurements or the ingredients of bread. Whenever discovered, such behaviour was ruthlessly punished by the authorities.

The pain of hunger drove some of the inhabitants to the extreme of human behaviour: cannibalism. Records document some 1,500 individual cases of cannibalism during the blockade. Mostly it was a case of persons cutting flesh or organs from people who had already died from starvation, but there were also instances of individuals actually being murdered for the foodstuff their corpses could provide. In a surprisingly large number of cases, the perpetrators were women – mothers driven to near-insanity in

a final attempt to get food for their starving children.

The struggle for survival changed people's outlook on life but their indomitable spirit carried them along. Despite the exhausting conditions, the citizens tried desperately to maintain some semblance of normality. Some university colleges continued to provide lectures and even took examinations during the siege. Theatres and concert halls opened occasionally and actors and musicians gave performances as best as they could, with both them and their audiences bundled up against the cold.

Chilling scenes showing the privations borne by the people of Leningrad. Food would be sought anywhere it could be found and water had to be hand-drawn no matter what the prevailing weather inflicted on them.
SSETO

Two frozen corpses beside the Summer Gardens. One has succumbed in a sitting position. (Novosti)

The northern fence of the Summer Gardens along the Neva river, photographed by Vladimir in the summer of 2003.

THE 'ROAD OF LIFE' – ACROSS LAKE LADOGA

WITH THE CITY sealed from the north by the Finns, from the south by the Germans and with the Gulf of Finland barred by enemy mines, the only access to the beleaguered city was across Lake Ladoga or by air. Some supplies were flown in by air-lift, but the quantities remained small. The Leningrad planners knew that the only way to get enough supplies into the city was by a route of some sort across Lake Ladoga.

Some 125 miles long and 80 miles wide, the lake reaches depths of up to 700 feet. Weather conditions vary considerably during the year. During the summer months ferocious storms can suddenly appear, while in winter low temperatures prevail and the waters can freeze to a considerable depth. The most difficult time for any movement across the lake is during spring and autumn when the ice is unstable.

As long as the lake did not freeze up, supplies could reach Leningrad by ship. Provisions could be brought up from the east by rail as far as Volkhov, 25 miles south of Lake Ladoga. Transferred onto transport vessels, the stores could then be sailed up the Volkhov river to the lake-side town of Novaya Ladoga and from there to Osinovets on the Leningrad side of the lake, from where a narrow-gauge railway line would carry them the last 35 miles to the

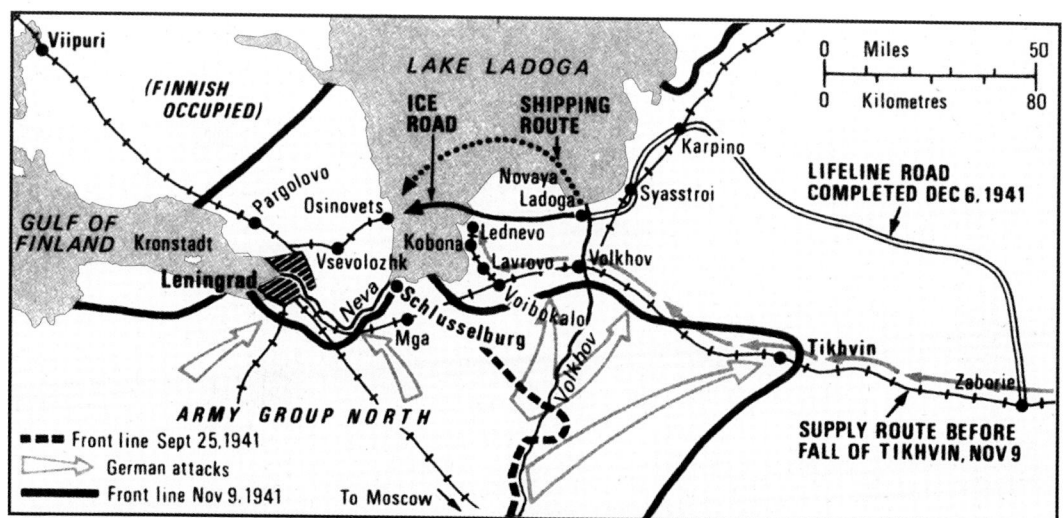

The ice road across Lake Ladoga – the 'Road of Life' – saved Leningrad from total starvation in the first winter of the siege.

city. Until early September ships had been able to sail right into the city via the Neva river, but this route became impossible when the Germans captured Schlüsselburg, which lies at the start of the river. From Schlüsselburg, German artillery was also able to harass rail traffic on the Osinovets line.

Preparations were quickly put in hand to arrange a shipping route across the lake, including the formation of special Lake Ladoga shipping flotilla. A formidable force of 20,000 workers was assembled and set to work constructing docks and warehouses at Kobona, Lavroro, Novaya Ladoga and Voibokalo on the southern shores of the lake and at Osinovets and Kokkorevo on the Leningrad side. The range of materials available severely limited the sophistication of the installations that were constructed but the Russian capability for improvisation quickly came to the fore and enough facilities were provided to make dispatch and reception of supplies feasible.

The first two ships arrived at Osinovets on 12th September, bringing in 800 tons of grain – less than was needed for just one day. Nevertheless, the news of the ships' arrival was received with great enthusiasm in Leningrad. Three large vessels, each carrying 1,000 tons of wheat, arrived on the 15th. While one was being unloaded, the other two were attacked by Stuka dive-bombers and sunk with all the foodstuff aboard. (The ships were later explored by divers and, although in most cases the grain aboard had become rotten, a few hundred tons of wheat were salvaged and declared usable.)

After that, ships would only sail after dark, and had to be escorted by Navy gunboats. Still, many did not survive the passage, 24 boats being sunk in the next four weeks. The shipping route lasted for a month before the onset of winter made further delivery by boat impossible. By then, some 45,000 tons of stores had been brought in, a considerable quantity but not nearly enough to meet the needs.

On 8th November, the 12. Panzer-Division of Schmidt's XXXIX Panzerkorps occupied the town of Tikhvin, some 100 miles east of Mga. The loss of Tikhvin was a major blow to the supply route organisers as the town lay on the railway line which handled the flow of supplies to Volkhov, the railhead for the shipping route across Lake Ladoga. The severing of the rail line made immediate re-routing necessary. Anticipating the fall of Tikhvin, the Leningrad authorities had already made plans for the construction of an entirely new road right through the swamps, bogs and dense timber forests north of the German salient to a point of embarkation on the lake still occupied by Russian forces. Moscow initially objected to the plans, which they thought would waste too many valuable resources, but after the fall of Tikhvin quickly approved. The proposed road would be 220 miles in length. It would start at Zaborye, 60 miles east of Tikhvin, and run first north to Lakhta, then west to Karpino, from where it would descend on Syasstroi on the south-east corner of Lake Ladoga, and from there onwards to Novaya Ladoga and Voibokalo. The road would be required to carry a minimum of 2,000 tons of supplies every day. Leningrad food officials estimated that, unless the road could be completed within two weeks, death by starvation would soon overtake everybody within the blockade.

The road would be built from west to east. An army of peasants and rear-area troops – men, women and children – was assembled and put to work, in freezing cold and deep snow, equipped with little more than picks, shovels and handsaws. They had a few army lorries and tractors for hauling timber but no bulldozers or snowploughs. Two tanks were available and these were used to pull down trees and to provide the materials needed to cross the swampy areas. Work continued night and day, the work site lit up by campfires that provided a little warmth for the labourers during breaks. What they built was not an all-weather tarmac road on a solid base with drainage but basically a cleared path through the forest with fascines laid down across streams and swamps, and timber bridges constructed where necessary. For most of its length it was just wide enough for one vehicle.

Meanwhile, knowing that the waters of Lake Ladoga would inevitably freeze, preparations also continued for the establishment of a supply route

As soon as ice conditions allowed, a scouting party was sent out to reconnoitre a suitable passage across the frozen lake. The route was staked out and opened for transport on 20th November but, with the ice still not thick enough to safely support trucks, the first convoy across was comprised of horse-drawn cargo sledges.

across the ice. Ice would normally begin to form sometime around mid-November, but in some years, substantial ice did not form until late January. Initially it was not known if it was feasible for a road to be built across the ice and carry the weight of motorised traffic. Experts determined that a thickness of seven inches (18cm) of ice was needed to support a horse and sledge with a one-ton load; eight inches (20cm) to carry a truck with a one-ton load; and one foot (30cm) to carry a whole convoy. One day of minus 15°C would create four inches of ice, eight days were needed to make a foot. Once formed, the ice could rapidly build up to a thickness of three to five feet which would carry any load and would last until the end of the winter.

Ice first began to form on the lake on 8th November. Every day, tests were carried out to measure its growing thickness.

An hour before dawn on 17th November – nine days after the fall of Tikhvin – two reconnaissance teams ventured out on the thin ice. One, led by A. N. Stafeyev, tested the ice in the vicinity of Osinovets and Kokkorevo, the two ports on the Leningrad side. The other, headed by Lieutenant Leonid Sokolov and with 30 men from the 88th Construction Battalion, set out across the Bay of Schlüsselburg, the narrowest part of the lake, to scout out a route from Kokkorevo to the island of Zelenets and on to Kobona on the eastern shore, 22 miles away. Their orders were to find a route that would be able to carry a horse and sledge with a load of 100 kilos. Making their way through barren cold and a blazing snowstorm, roped together in order not to get separated, some of them wearing life belts, the team drove on. Every hundred yards they stopped to drill a measuring hole in the ice and leave a flagged route-marker pole in it. Forced to find detours around open spots and ice-floes, they slowly but doggedly made their way across the white expanse. Well after midnight, after some 20 hours on the ice, they reached Kobona.

Their report that a route could be opened was quickly telephoned back to Leningrad. Their superior, Major A. S. Mozhayev, immediately set out on his horse and, following the flagged route, reached Kobona in four hours. Next day, 19th November, Lieutenant-General F. N. Lagunov, the man in charge of the ice road, drove a light scout car across the ice from Kokkorevo to Kobona – the first motorised vehicle to cross.

Though the ice was still thin and unreliable, the authorities decided to take the risk and ordered the road to be opened. On 20th November, a convoy of horses with sledges and 350 drivers under Captain Mikal Murov crossed the lake to Kobona, then returned early next morning, each sleigh carrying about 100 kilos of flour and dried food. With the city having a daily need of 3,000 tons it was only a drop in the ocean of the city's requirements, but the important thing was that it proved that it could be done. The first motor convoy crossed on the evening of 22nd November, 60 lorries bringing 33 tons of flour on the 23rd. That first week the 'Road of Life', as the Leningraders dubbed the lake road, delivered 736 tons of food to the city – a considerable quantity but not nearly enough to save the population from starvation.

By 22nd November, the ice was one-foot thick, strong enough to support motor transport. However, there were still many weak spots and at least forty trucks went to the bottom in the first week alone. In order not to crack the ice, trucks had to maintain a speed not much faster than walking pace and keep a safe distance between vehicles, although both these limitations decreased as the ice grew thicker. In due course an elaborate network of guides, traffic-control posts (one every 200 or 300 yards), repair depots, feeding points, communications, rescue, first-aid stations and road-defence positions was created along the various routes. In all, some 19,000 people were employed in the ice-road operation, working in temperatures averaging 20 to 40 degrees below zero.

A female traffic officer stands guard at the gate-like structure that was erected to indicate the beginning of the 'Road of Life'. In an effort to increase deliveries, from January 1942 truck drivers attempted to speed up their journeys, 261 of them achieving two round trips per day that month. During March, 355 of them make three trips and 100 even managed to complete five.

With more routes being opened, the ice road was organised as a two-way, round-the-clock transport system. Although it increased the risk of enemy shelling or air bombardment, the often dismal weather conditions on the lake and the short hours of daylight necessitated many truck convoys to travel with blazing headlights. Boris Kudoyarov pictured one such convoy passing two lone traffic regulators on the barren, icy plain. (Novosti)

As the ice thickened, more and more trails were opened across the lake. By mid-winter there were as many as 60. All between 22 and 25 miles long, they ran across the Bay of Schlüsselburg from either Lavrovo, Kobona or Lednevo on the eastern shore to either Kokkorevo, Vaganovo and Osinovets on the Leningrad side.

Meanwhile, work on the emergency road to Zaborye had progressed steadily. On 6th December, the road reached the end of the forest and was pushed on to the rail terminus at Zaborye where, within minutes of its completion, the first convoy of trucks was on the move with supplies to the city. However, the poor state of the hastily-constructed road soon took its toll. Within three hours the leading vehicle got stuck, holding up the entire convoy for hours before it could be dug out. This scenario repeated itself countless times. The trek soon turned into chaos. Trucks bogged down, slid into swamps, or were hit by German artillery. The convoy took six days to reach Lednevo. Driving at walking pace, they needed another 27 hours to cross Lake Ladoga. A total of 350 trucks were lost in this first convoy, but badly needed supplies had again reached the city.

After so much toil and endeavour, it was an ironic twist of fate that on 9th December – only three days after completion of the road and only a month after the occupation of Tikhvin had dictated its construction – Tikhvin was recaptured by the Soviet 4th Army under General Kirill A. Meretskov after a pitched battle. Realising its vital importance, Schmidt's XXXIX Panzerkorps fiercely defended the town, losing over 7,000 troops in their attempt to hold

Heavy snowfalls made continuous clearing of the road necessary. In all, the Leningrad Front road service removed snow from 1,375 miles of road surface. In due course, the high snow embankments built up alongside the road formed a buffer against the snowstorms and gales blowing on the frozen expanse. The snow walls also served to indicate the route, enabling the number of road guides and traffic-control points to be reduced.

it. The recapture of Tikhvin meant that supply trains could again reach Volkhov, the rail terminal for Novaya Ladoga, which would considerably speed up delivery to Leningrad, and make the long truck haul through the forest superfluous.

The news that Tikhvin was back in Russian hands greatly boosted morale in the beleaguered city. Coming on the 70th day of the siege, it was the first positive sign that the city could perhaps be saved and the enemy defeated. Yet it took considerable time before the rail terminals could actually be used again as the Germans had destroyed numerous bridges, warehousing and storage facilities during their retreat. While these were being repaired, it was still necessary to use the forest road to supply the eastern lakeside depots. Using German equipment that had been captured in the fighting, the Soviets widened and strengthened the road. A quantity of German petrol captured at Tikhvin helped to keep the trucks moving.

Yet, the amount of stores delivered to Leningrad across the frozen lake was depressingly low. The journey across the ice remained slow and dangerous. Trucks, and their drivers, frequently disappeared through the ice or were lost in the blizzards. Maintenance of the truck fleet was a nightmare as there was a wide variety of vehicles involved and a constant lack of spare parts. Petrol was in short supply and of very poor quality. Enemy action also caused disruptions: there was almost continuous shelling, aerial bombing and even commando-style raids across the ice. Unremitting fighting in the Volkhov region caused considerable damage to the supply terminals. The single-track railway between Ladoga and Leningrad suffered from broken-down engines, lack of fuel, along with personnel being equally susceptible to starvation.

However, despite all its shortcomings, the system continued to work. By 23rd December, the ice road had brought in 16,449 tons of food – an average of 361 tons a day. By now, rail traffic to Volkhov was such that the operation of the forest road could be wound down. On 25th December, although there was still little more than two days' supply of flour on hand, Zhdanov decided to raise the daily bread rations for the first time since the start of the siege: workers now received 350 grams – 100 grams more than before; all the others got 200 – an increase of 75 grams. That same day, the forest road was decommissioned.

On 31st December, the Soviets recaptured the little railway town of Voibokalo, 40 miles west of Volkhov and that much closer to the starting points of the ice routes across the Bay of Schlüsselburg. The next day, New Year's Day 1942, the first supply train from Tikhvin rolled into town. An endless procession of trucks began shuttling from there back and forth across the frozen lake, sometimes as much as 400 a day. In an attempt to further increase deliveries, the truck drivers organised a competition as to who could make the fastest delivery run. In January, workers built a new railway branch from Voibokalo to Kobona, thereby shortening the journey of the trucks by another 25 miles. By the end of January, 1,500 tons of supplies were reaching Leningrad every day.

The returning trucks also began bringing citizens out of the city. Right from the beginning of the siege, people had begun to leave their beleaguered homesteads. Some 33,500 persons had been lucky enough to get a place on the boats in the autumn, and another 35,000 had been flown out in November-December. Many others had tried the long and difficult walk across the frozen lake or hitch-hiked a lift on one of the returning trucks. Thousands had frozen to death on the ice, but by 22nd January, 1942, some 36,000 had come out this way. That day, the city authorities decreed the evacuation of one quarter of the remaining population: 500,000 people. Priority was given to the elderly and children, but many adults were allowed to go too. Anyone evacuated from the encircled city meant one mouth fewer to feed. In the last ten days of January the trucks brought out 11,000; in February 117,000; in March 221,000; in April 163,000. By the end of April, more than half a million civilians had left the city, and only 110,000 remained.

Gradually, very gradually, conditions within the city improved. On 24th January, the daily bread rations were increased again: 400 grams for workers, 300 for employees, 250 for dependents and children. On 11th February, they were raised again, to 500, 400 and 300 grams respectively. However, for thousands of Leningraders the improvement in the supply situation came too late. After months of slow starvation, it was impossible

In the spring of 1942, to prevent the outbreak of infectious disease, the city authorities mobilised the population for a massive clean-up operation. Between 27th March and 15th April, over 300,000 people worked to remove vermin and garbage from streets, homes, buildings and waterways. The operation covered three million square metres of streets and 16,000 buildings, and resulted in the disposal of a million tons of refuse. Here, citizens clear Liteiny Prospect of snow. (Novosti)

The same street – pristine and sparkling – pictured by Vladimir in the summer of 2003.

to nurse those that were already fading back to health, and they still succumbed to the effects of malnutrition.

The besieged were also killed by enemy action. During the first three months of 1942 alone over 14,800 shells fell on the city, killing 519 and wounding 1,447. Such actions continued throughout the length of the siege until the German forces withdrew out of range of the city.

The winter of 1941-42 was by far the worst period of the 900-day siege. The cost in human lives was staggering. Exact figures are difficult to come by. The official figure announced by the Soviet Government after the war, minimised for political reasons, was that 641,803 had died from starvation and 29,832 been killed by enemy shelling, air raids and other war causes, making for a total death toll of 671,673. But these figures are evidently incomplete and present-day Russian historians estimate that of the three and a half million people present inside the city perimeter (including Kronstadt and the Oranienbaum enclave) at the start of the siege, between 1.3 and 1.5 million died.

As spring arrived, the city appeared to gain a new lease of life. Though still feeble from hunger and exhaustion, the population went out to get city life back on its feet. Zhdanov issued a decree calling on every citizen

To increase the food reserves, the city authorities also instituted a campaign to grow vegetables on any suitable piece of land. These cabbages are being harvested in the park on St Isaac's Square – seen earlier on page 32. (Novosti)

St Isaac's Square today, with the corner of the Astoria Hotel on the left and looking into Bolshaya Morskaya Street.

The 'Road of Life' – Across Lake Ladoga • 73

Another picture taken in the same park shows a Red Army officer admiring the rich harvest. In all, over 2,000 hectares of land were planted inside the blockade area in 1942, producing 76,000 tons of vegetables. (Novosti)

The southern façade of St Isaac's Cathedral makes for an easy comparison.

between 15 and 60 to do his bit. Streets were cleared of snow, dirt and debris; roofs and windows repaired. Corpses uncovered by the melting snow were taken away to be buried. Water and sewage mains were repaired, power stations brought back in order. Any pieces of land that could be brought into cultivation – parks, gardens, empty plots – were taken into use to grow vegetables, potatoes and other foodstuff. On 15th April, the first trams re-appeared on the streets.

Almost as a symbol of Leningrad's indomitable spirit, on 9th April the Leningrad Philharmonic Orchestra performed Dmitri D. Shostakovich's Seventh Symphony, for the first time. The piece was christen the Leningrad Symphony. It was performed in front of a packed house. (The famous Leningrad composer had worked on the piece inside the besieged city until October, refusing to be evacuated until the authorities ordered him to. He had finished the symphony at Kuibyshev, where it had also premiered in March.)

With the advance of spring, the melting ice on Lake Ladoga meant the advent of another critical period in the supply situation. Feverishly, the city authorities strove to build up reserves to bridge the gap between the end of the ice road and the resumption of the supply by shipping. By the time the road was closed – on 24th April – Leningrad had built up reserves of flour for

Periods of thaw severely limited vehicular movement in December. The onset of the spring thaw heralded the final end, but everything was done to keep the lake road open as long as possible. Pools of water and cracks in the ice forced a first curtailment of traffic on 25th March 1942; bus traffic was halted on 15th April; tanker trucks could no longer cross after 19th April; and the order to halt all movement across the ice was issued on 21st April. Yet a final convoy made it to Leningrad on 24th April, the cargo comprising 65 tons of spring onions!

58 days, cereals for 57 days, meat and fish for 140 days, fats for 123 days and sugar for 90 days.

As soon as the waters of Lake Ladoga were again navigable, the Russians resumed supply by shipping. The cargo ships were protected by a Navy flotilla consisting of three gunboats, the destroyer Konstruktor, about 20 patrol boats and some smaller craft fitted out with tank turrets. The Germans tried disrupting the supply lines, attacking the convoys with armed Siebel ferries. Assistance arrived on 22nd June in the form of four Italian MAS torpedo boats, which destroyed one of the Soviet gunboats on 15th August and sank a 1,300-ton supply lighter. The Finns had a gunboat flotilla on the lake too, but in general they restricted themselves to patrolling. In all, the Russians lost about 124 ships of various types on the lake, though overall their defence of the supply routes was a success.

The ice road memorial at Vaganovo on the Leningrad side of the lake.

1942: FAILED ATTEMPTS TO LIFT THE SIEGE

AWARE OF ITS symbolical value, Stalin and the Stavka were determined to lift the blockade of Leningrad. Twice in 1942, the Red Army launched a large-scale offensive in an attempt to relieve the city. Both failed miserably.

In January, as part of the Red Army's general winter offensive along the entire Eastern Front, three Soviet army groups – from north to south: Lieutenant-General M. S. Khozin's Leningrad Front, Meretskov's Volkhov Front and Colonel-General P. A. Kurochkin's North-Western Front – were to launch an ambitious attack. The aim was to cut off and destroy German forces in the Mga and Liuban sectors and restore communications with Leningrad. The main effort was to be made by Meretskov's Volkhov Front. Its 2nd Shock and 59th Armies were to attack north-westwards from the Volkhov river and capture Liuban and Chudovo prior to an advance towards Leningrad. To their south, Meretskov's own 52nd Army and the 11th Army of Kurochkin's North-Western Front were to support this main effort by capturing Novgorod. Kurochkin's other three armies further south – the 34th, 3rd and 4th Shock armies – were to take Demiansk and cut off the German withdrawal routes. In the north, Khozin's Leningrad Front would support the main effort by having its 54th Army attack south-westwards from the Volkhov river and its 55th Army south-eastwards from the Leningrad perimeter. If the latter army linked up with the 54th Army and the Volkhov Front armies coming up from the south, the blockade would be broken. As events transpired, this was a big 'if'.

Delayed by the weather, and with many of the assault and support units not yet in place, the Volkhov Front offensive jumped off on 6th January. Committed piecemeal, the 59th Army (Major-General I. V. Galanin) and 2nd Shock Army (Lieutenant-General G. G. Sokolov) suffered heavy initial losses amid the Germans' strong forward defences and bogged down in confusion after two days. After regrouping, the attack was resumed on the 13th with the 2nd Shock Army (now led by Lieutenant-General N. K. Klykov) leading. On the 17th, Klykov finally penetrated the German defences and in heavy fighting managed to advance six miles.

Faced with the Soviet penetration south-east of Leningrad, von Leeb asked Hitler for permission to withdraw his Heeresgruppe Nord forces to a more coherent defence line. When Hitler refused, Von Leeb handed in his resignation. On 18th January, Hitler replaced him with von Küchler. The

Generaloberst Georg von Küchler.
(SSETO)

latter's place as commander of the 18. Armee was taken by Generaloberst Georg Lindemann.

On 24th January, Meretskov launched his mechanised exploitation force, which brought the 2nd Shock Army forward another 45 miles, to a position south of Liuban. More than 100,000 Soviet troops were now in the German rear area, threatening to cut off the German forces in the north.

However, Busch's 16. Armee in the south and Lindemann's 18. Armee in the north, robustly managed to contain the enemy penetration, and, although the 2nd Shock Army doggedly continued its attempts to capture Liuban. By late February the Volkhov Front offensive in this area had come to a standstill. On 15th March, Küchler's 18. Armee launched a strong counter-attack and, battling through heavy resistance, managed to cut the narrow supply corridor to the 2nd Shock Army, which then became trapped in the frozen swampy wastelands south of Liuban. The Soviets desperately fought to re-open the supply routes, but by the end of April the 2nd Shock Army was inexorably cut off. Short

A German machine-gun post with the troops wrapped up against the cold as the winter starts to set in. Behind them a Soviet T-26S stands abandoned. (SSETO)

German grenadiers relax whilst out of the front line at Leningrad. Their faces portray the grim reality of war on the eastern front. (SSETO)

of ammunition, food and supplies (and led since 20th April by yet another commander, Lieutenant-General Andrei A. Vlasov), it fought on for another two months, launching several, increasingly desperate attempts to break out. In mid-June, the Volkhov Front made several attempts to liberate the encircled army but all failed. By early July, the 18. Armee had destroyed the 2nd Shock Army, capturing some 48,000 troops, including General Vlasov.

Meanwhile, the supporting offensive by the Leningrad Front in the north had failed as well. Its 54th Army (Major-General Ivan I. Fedyuninsky) attacked on 4th January (two days before the main offensive), but within two days was thrown back to its jumping-off positions. Resuming the attack on the 13th, it

1942: Failed attempts to lift the seige • 79

By now a familiar sight with the Gostiny Dvor bazaar on the right and the Russian National Library in the far background.

Although the Soviet offensives mounted in 1942 did not bring the hoped-for raising of the siege, these counter-strokes tied down German troops and attracted large German forces away from southern Russia at a time when the Wehrmacht was waging its summer offensive in the Caucasus towards Stalingrad. The Leningrad, Volkhov and North-Western Fronts suffered staggering losses, but inflicted considerable damage on the Wehrmacht too. On 25th July 1942, Boris Kudoyarov pictured a group of German prisoners being marched along Nevsky Prospect. (Novosti)

captured Pogoste on the 17th, but frustratingly could go no further. Once more renewing its offensive on 4th March, Fedyunisky's army managed to advance to within six miles of Liuban before it was halted for good and became locked in a fruitless struggle around Smerdynia. Leningrad Front's other armies, scheduled to attack from within the Leningrad perimeter, were simply too weak to make any impression or progress at all.

The supporting offensive by the North-Western Front in the south achieved more, but also fell short of its ambitious targets. Attacking on 7th January, its armies penetrated the German defences and by 26th February had encircled the II Armeekorps in Demiansk. However, despite prolonged attempts from 6th March until 9th April, they were unable to crush the encircled corps, which defended itself skilfully and was re-supplied from the air. Worse still, on 20th March, a German relieving force of five divisions advanced east from Staraia Russa and linked up with the trapped force the following day. The North-Western Front attacked incessantly but could not close the corridor, and the offensive in this sector ground to a halt around 20th May.

After five months of intense fighting in difficult terrain and appalling weather conditions, the Soviet winter offensive to relieve Leningrad had failed spectacularly. The campaigns in Volkhov, Leningrad and the North-Western Front together lost nearly 554,000 men killed, captured or missing – the siege of the city had not been lifted.

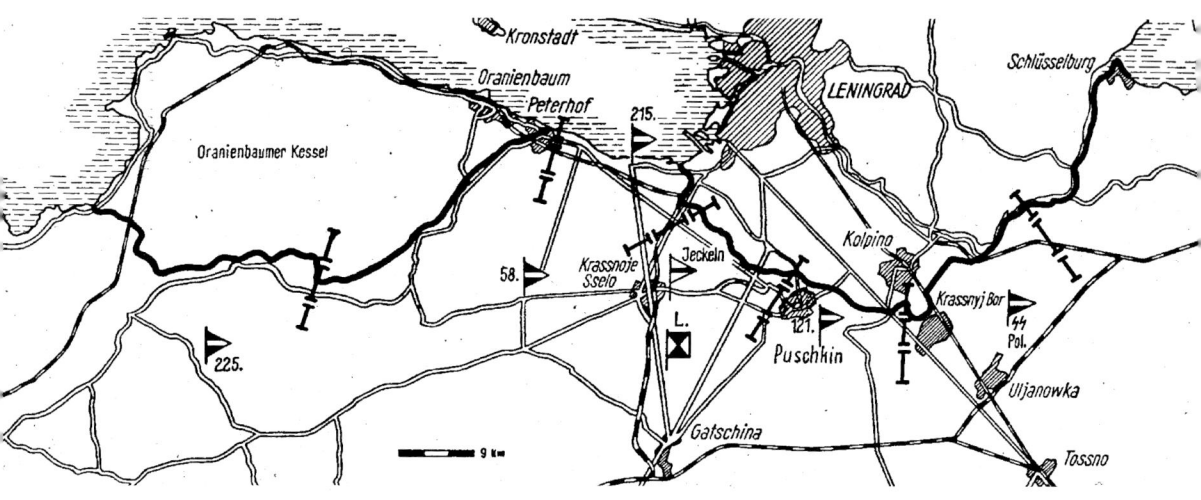

By early October 1941 the Germans had completed their encircling manoeuvres around Leningrad and around the Oranienbaum pocket to the west and had started consolidating their positions. From then on until January 1943 the front lines in this sector remained largely static, with both sides dug in, practically the only change being the rotation of units. This map shows the German order of battle as it was in August 1942, when the L Armeekorps was holding the line, with the 225. and 58. Infanterie-Divisions containing the 'Oranienbaumer Kessel' (Oranienbaum Cauldron) and the 215. Infanterie-Division, Kampfgruppe Jeckeln (comprising Flemish, Norwegian and Dutch SS Volunteer Legions), the 121. Infanterie-Division and the SS-Polizei-Division occupying the encirclement line south of Leningrad.

State propaganda took every opportunity to bolster morale and to push the Communist Party line. Here a noticeboard, resplendent in party imagery, the clear intention being that successes are associated with the Party. The sign reads: 'Messages to the heroic defenders of Leningrad.' SSETO

In the summer, both sides made plans for new offensives. In July, Hitler sent urgently needed reinforcements to the Leningrad sector designed to complete the total envelopment of the city and secure its final reduction. These included Generalfeldmarschall von Manstein's 11. Armee, fresh from its victories in the Crimea, with four divisions, and its specialist, super-heavy siege artillery. The 11. Armee was charged with planning an attack to the north-east to finally effect a link-up with the Finnish forces in an operation called Nordlicht, the super-heavy siege mortars were to pummel Kronstadt to ruins.

Noticing the German build-up, Stalin and the Stavka ordered the Leningrad and Volkhov Fronts to conduct a large-scale offensive to pre-empt the expected German offensive and, if possible, lift the blockade. The sector chosen for the attack was the German Mga – Schlüsselburg salient south of Lake Ladoga. The two army groups planned a concentric attack, with the Leningrad Front led by Lieutenant-General Leonid A. Govorov, launching its 55th Army and the Neva Operational Group towards the east, and the Volkhov Front, under Meretskov, its 8th Army and a reconstituted 2nd Shock Army to the west.

Better organised than its predecessor, and given more armour and artillery support, the Volkhov Front offensive started on 27th August. The attack caught the Germans by surprise. Major-General F. N. Starikov's 8th Army managed to drive forward some ten miles to Siniavino, just four miles short of the Leningrad perimeter lines along the Neva.

Reacting quickly to this threat to the blockade, Küchler sent one division after another to oppose the penetration, five in all, among them four earmarked for Operation 'Nordlicht'. Heavy fighting developed around Siniavino. The Soviets managed to crawl another two miles closer to Leningrad but by 3rd September, their attack was faltering.

The Leningrad Front had made an initial attack across the Neva on 19th August, which had made little headway. Now, with the Volkhov Front spearheads so close, Govorov launched the 55th Army (Major-General V. P. Sviridov) and the Neva Operational Group across the Neva

Another propaganda hoarding, this time more visceral. 'Kill Germans', it proclaims at the top. Under the poster of the two patriots standing over the body of a woman it reads, 'Revenge!' SSETO

1942: Failed attempts to lift the seige • **83**

One remarkable story to come out of the siege was the use of the city's blind citizens as part of the air defences. Thanks to the efforts of the blind musician, Vladimir Karolenko, it was discovered that the visually impaired were often particularly sensitive to sound. Volunteers were sought and a group was selected, then trained to operate the city's aircraft listening equipment. They were each paired with a sighted soldier, to act as their eyes for using the equipment. Their ability to detect incoming air raids much earlier than normally sighted trained crews was unquestionable. So keen were Leningrad's blind to serve in this capacity that the authorities could be quite selective as to who was recruited. After training it was found that they were often able to detect the different engine notes of particular German aircraft, which then had a bearing on how the air defences were deployed. SSETO

in an attempt to link up with Meretskov. None of these attacks got very far and on the 12th, the assault forces were ordered to withdraw to their starting positions.

An exasperated Hitler ordered von Manstein and his 11. Armee to restore the situation and neutralise the Soviet offensive. On 10th September, Manstein's initial counter-attack, with one panzer and two infantry divisions, was stopped short by enemy artillery, mortars and minefields. A more-carefully-planned pincer attack on the 21st had more success, and by the 25th had encircled both the Soviet 8th and 2nd Shock Armies. The Leningrad

Front launched relief attacks across the Neva but these were quickly thrown back by the Germans. In heavy fighting from 30th September to 15th October Manstein's army systematically reduced the Siniavino pocket, although the bulk of the two Russian armies managed to escape from it.

Although they all failed to raise the blockade, the Soviet offensives of 1942 did at least prevent the Germans from completing the total envelopment of Leningrad. All German plans for a drive to finally link up with the Finns were disrupted by the Russian attacks. German reinforcements sent north for such an attack had to be committed and were spent staving off the Soviet offensives.

The winter of 1942-43, Leningrad's second winter under siege, was not nearly as bad as the first and caused far fewer casualties. Several factors combined to prevent another period of starvation. Firstly, and most tragically, because of the previous year's death toll and the continued evacuations from the city, the population was now much smaller than a year earlier. Since May another 449,000 civilians had been brought out, so that by November, Leningrad needed to feed only 700,000 citizens and some 420,000 soldiers. Secondly, far greater food reserves had been amassed in the city. Thirdly, the winter of 1942-43 was thankfully significantly less severe than that of the previous year. Lake Ladoga froze up much later, enabling supply by cargo ships to continue until 27th November, and in the northern parts of the lake, where the ice formed later, even until 7th January, 1943. Fourthly, the authorities now knew much better how to organise the ice road. Opened on 19th December, the road functioned, with some interruptions due to weak ice, until 30th March and in this period transported over 210,000 tons of cargo, mainly food and ammunition, transporting more than 200,000 personnel and evacuees. And lastly, in mid-January the Red Army finally succeeded in breaking the blockade.

Living conditions for the population of Leningrad were grim, especially for the children. A semi-subterranean existence became quite normal and basements became homes, schools, and factories. SSETO

1942: Failed attempts to lift the seige • 85

1943: THE BLOCKADE IS BROKEN

IN EARLY 1943, the Soviets made new plans for an offensive that was to lift the siege. The German setbacks at Stalingrad caused Hitler to move most of the 11. Armee southwards again. This weakening of the front around Leningrad gave the Soviets the opportunity they had been waiting for. This time they concentrated their attack where the German ring around the city was at its narrowest: south of Lake Ladoga between Mga and Schlüsselburg.

On 18th January 1943, the Red Army finally broke the siege of Leningrad when it opened a land corridor into the city from the east. Railway connections were quickly restored and on 7th February, the first train, its engine decorated with pictures of Stalin and Molotov and texts hailing the 'heroism of the people of Leningrad in the struggle against the German Fascists', rolled into Finland Station.

Although the first train is recorded as having been pulled by Loco No. L-1208 and the original picture shows it to have three steam domes, it is another locomotive, No. 3721-83 with two domes, that has been preserved as a memorial to this event at Petrokrepost Railway Station on the north shore of the Neva at Oreshek/Schlüsselburg. (R. Hogg)

The German salient along the Neva river at this point was only 15 miles wide. The plan — code-named Operation 'Iskra' (Spark) — was for a concentric attack by two army groups, Govorov's Leningrad Front attacking from the blockaded city eastwards, and Meretskov's Volkhov Front attacking westwards towards it.

The simultaneous attack began on 12th January. After a massive artillery preparation and supported by some 400 aircraft, the 67th Army (Lieutenant-General Mikhail P. Dukhanov) made an assault-crossing of the Neva river and struck eastward with eight rifle divisions plus five rifle, two ski and three tank brigades. Similarly supported, the 2nd Shock Army (Lieutenant-General V. Z. Romanovsky) pushed west with 11 rifle divisions, one rifle, two ski and four tank brigades. Both armies made rapid progress, overwhelming and pushing aside the German 170. and 227. Infanterie-Divisions, and by the end of the first day had covered about one-third of the distance that separated them. The 18. Armee rushed reinforcements up from the south — combat groups of the 61. and 96. Infanterie-Divisions, 5. Gebirgsjäger-Division and the SS-Polizei-Division — in a desperate attempt to hold the salient, but the Soviet offensive was too strong. On 18th January, the two armies achieved contact, the first link-up being made by the 67th Army's 123rd Rifle Division and the 2nd Shock Army's 372nd Rifle Division

Long queues formed whenever meagre rations could be sourced by shops. SSETO

just east of Workers Settlement No. 1. The Soviets swiftly moved in troops to reinforce the precariously narrow opening, building up a strong shield to the south.

The blockade of Leningrad had been broken. For the first time in 16 months the city was again in overland contact with the outside world. All of Leningrad rejoiced at the news. Engineers began immediate work to restore railway connections with the city, building a new railway bridge across the Neva at Schlüsselburg. On 7th February, the first freight train rolled into Finland Station, welcomed by a huge crowd of happy citizens. Finally, a steady supply of food and munitions to the city was secure. No longer the city needed to rely on the erratic delivery across Lake Ladoga. It was a decisive turning point in the battle.

On 22nd February, the city rations could be increased again, to 700 grams for industrial workers, 600 grams for other workers, 500 for employees and 400 for dependents and children. With the railway operating it not only became possible to bring in food, but also heavy machinery and materials to commence war production. During the blockade, manufacture of some tanks, mines, small arms, shells, artillery and grenades had continued while materials were still available, but this was only a small part of the city's potential. Now, full-scale manufacture could be resumed.

But although the blockade had been broken, the siege continued.

Leningrad and the Oranienbaum enclave still lay within easy range of the German artillery guns, and German bombers could still penetrate the city. German troops were still dug in within sight of the city centre. All through 1943, bombs and shells would continue to rain down on the city, and add thousands of victims to the already endless list of casualties.

Russian submarines operating in the Gulf of Finland from Kronstadt had achieved some modest successes in 1942, including the sinking of SS Argo and 23 ships of various types. In order to contain the submarine threat, the Germans and Finns decided to construct a barrier across the entrance to the Gulf to supplement the minefields. A major feat of engineering, the barrier consisted of two rows of steel netting almost 65 miles long laid directly across the gulf between Porkkala in Finland and an island west of Tallinn in Estonia. Suspended to a depth of over 200 feet, the nets had 8,454 mines positioned between them. Some 140 surface ships took part in the building project. Completed in April 1943, the barrage proved extremely successful and during 1943 not one Russian submarine managed to gain passage through the Gulf to the Baltic. At least three Russian submarines are known to have been destroyed in the barrage and several were damaged after making repeated attempts to penetrate it.

A temporary wall has been erected across this street with the crudely scrawled message, Danger – Unexploded Bomb. SSETO

1944: END OF THE SIEGE

WITH THE LIFTING of the blockade, and the easing-up of the supply situation in the city, it also became possible to build up military strength for the final offensive that would finally raise the siege of the city and throw back the Germans for good. All through 1943, trainloads of fresh troops and weapons arrived in Leningrad. Under great secrecy, the 2nd Shock Army was brought into the Oranienbaum enclave to the west of the city, troops and supplies arriving by ship or, after the onset of winter, across the frozen ice of the Gulf.

By autumn the planning for the breakout was complete. The new offensive was to be a huge pincer movement by two army groups. Govorov's Leningrad Front would attack with two armies, the 2nd Shock Army from the Oranienbaum enclave and the 42nd Army from the Pulkovo Heights on the southern edge of Leningrad (Operation 'Neva'). Both attacks would have full support of the Baltic Fleet guns and numerous rail-mounted guns. After meeting up, the two armies would sweep southwards. Meanwhile, some 120 miles to the south-east of Leningrad, Meretskov's Volkhov Front would launch its 59th Army and Southern Operational Group in a double attack across the Volkhov river north and south of Novgorod. Once that city had been enveloped, Meretskov would sweep westwards. If all went according to plan, the converging army groups would trap and destroy the German 18. Armee. The Soviets built up a substantial superiority over their German adversaries: Govorov had a majority of three to one in infantry, four to one in artillery, and six to one in tanks and aircraft; Meretskov outnumbered the Germans by three to one in infantry and eleven to one in armour.

The Germans, knowing full well that an attack was only a matter of time, had constructed a formidable system of defence fortifications to a depth of nearly 200 miles. The main line, known as the 'Panther Position', lay 150 miles south-west of Leningrad and included 6,000 bunkers, 140 miles of barbed-wire obstacles, tank ditches, etc. It was considered to be impregnable.

The Soviet offensive started on 14th January, 1944. Due to fog, supporting aircraft of the 13th Air Army could not take off. Nevertheless, after a preliminary bombardment by 6,000 guns, including the powerful guns of the Baltic Fleet batteries and ships, the 2nd Shock Army (Lieutenant-General I. I. Fedyuninsky) struck out from Oranienbaum across a six-mile-wide front. The 9. and 10. Luftwaffen-Feld-Divisions crumbled under the massed assault. By the evening the Soviets had penetrated two miles into the German defences.

Next day, 15th January, the 42nd Army (Colonel-General I. I. Maslennikov) struck out from Leningrad. The weather had cleared, enabling Soviet aircraft to assist the artillery in battering the German defences. By evening the 42nd Army had also advanced some three miles.

The Germans were initially not very worried by the Soviet penetrations, having failed to detect the massive power and reserve built up by their opponents. However, the 18. Armee had not enough men to fill the gaps and by 17th January, the 2nd Shock Army's breach was 15 miles wide and five miles deep. Late on 18th January, the two Soviet armies linked up just south of Ropsha, trapping the German forces still fighting in the north. Next day the 42nd Army took Krasnoye Selo, overrunning the German artillery positions that had rained down death and destruction on Leningrad for

A picture taken near the Detskoye Selo railway station in Pushkin, fifteen kilometres to the south of Leningrad on 21st January 1944. By this point the German 18. Armee was in full retreat. These troops are engaged in clearing the last vestiges of the surviving German units. SSETO

On 14th January 1944 the Red Army's Leningrad Front launched a massed offensive to finally drive the Wehrmacht away from Leningrad and bring the city out of reach of the German artillery. Attacking from the Oranienbaum enclave to the west of the city, the 2nd Shock Army blasted through the German lines. One of the places they occupied was Peterhof, the great ensemble of palaces founded by Tsar Peter the Great on the southern shores of the Gulf of Finland. Having lain just east of the Oranienbaum pocket and almost in the front line for 28 months, the palaces had suffered heavily, not least from German demolitions. Here cavalry soldiers inspect the ruined shell of the Great Palace and the famous Grand Cascade below it. (Novosti)

nearly two and a half years. A total of 85 artillery pieces were captured intact, and immediately turned against the retreating enemy.

In the south, the attack by the 59th Army (Lieutenant-General I. T. Korovnikov) and the Southern Operational Group (Major-General T. A.

Superbly rebuilt by the Russian restoration experts, the Great Palace has regained all of its former glory. Its Germanic name replaced in 1944 by the Russian equivalent Petrodovets, the palace officially reverted to its former name of Peterhof in 1992 (although the nearby town itself is still called Petrodovets). (R. Hogg)

Sviklin) had also started on 14th January. The assaults across the Volkhov river and the northern end of Lake Ilmen were hindered by the thaw and the difficult terrain. Many tanks got stuck in the riverside mud, and many vehicles and horse transports broke through the melting ice. Several times, von Küchler asked Hitler for permission to pull back the troops defending Novgorod, but each time the Führer refused. By 19th January, the Soviets had nearly closed the ring around the city, and the German XXXVIII Armeekorps was desperately clinging on to a narrow corridor out to the west. At the last hour, Hitler relented to von Küchler's requests and the German troops managed to escape under cover of darkness, leaving Novgorod a desolate wasteland of blasted ruins.

The German front collapsed. All along the line, the 18. Armee was now retreating to the Panther Position. By 27th January, the Germans had been

1944: End of the Siege • 93

During their two-and-a-half-year occupation the Germans had thoroughly plundered the Pushkin palaces and the fighting of 1944 further ruined the buildings and the town. Decades of restoration work have now repaired the exterior but much work remains to be done. Tsarskoye Selo was renamed Pushkin by the Communists in 1937 after the poet Alexander Pushkin.

One day after the 2nd Shock Army's attack from Oranienbaum, the 42nd Army attacked from Leningrad proper, striking southward to achieve the planned encirclement of German forces in that area. By 23rd January its CX Rifle Corps had enveloped Pushkin — the former Tsarskoye Selo (Royal Village), the 'Russian Versailles' housing the Imperial Palaces of Catherine and Alexander seventeen miles south of Leningrad. Having held on to the town and the two palaces for nine days but now encircled from three sides, the German 215. Infanterie-Division managed to escape southwards during the night of 23rd/24th January. In this staged photograph, Soviet soldiers charge through one of the gates of the Catherine Palace. (Novosti)

pushed back so far that even their farthest-reaching artillery guns could no longer reach Leningrad. The announcement to the population, over the city's public speaker system, caused an outburst of jubilation on the streets. It was the final end of the siege. A total of 876 days had gone by since the first shell fell on the city on 4th September 1941. That night, 324 guns fired a salute of 20 shots each to celebrate the deliverance of the city. The 900 days of Leningrad were over.

CONCLUSION

THE SIEGE OF Leningrad highlighted the folly of dogmatic adherence to a political imperative. During the earlier phase of the encirclement, Soviet forces seemed incapable of mounting an effective counter-attack, rigidly conforming to ideological diktat rather than evolving a coherent tactical plan. Later, as roles were reversed, the Germans suffered from political interference which dictated that ground of little strategic importance be held for what

The 'Monument to the Heroic Defenders of Leningrad' stands in Victory Square, at the southern end of Moscow Prospect. Here on 8th July 1945, the troops of the former Leningrad Front entered the city marching through a specially erected triumphal arch to take part in the victory parade. The monument was unveiled in 1975.
Vladimir Skvortsov

was, in effect, some imagined prestige. The fact that this compromised the Wehrmacht's ability to fight effectively held little importance for an increasingly remote and isolated Führer. Little has been made in this account of the predicament faced by the ordinary German soldiers who were besieging Leningrad. For the most part they would have been rotated out of the line regularly and so would have been able to recuperate somewhat. Until the latter half of 1943, they were not unduly challenged militarily by the defenders and seemed perfectly capable of fending off whatever was thrown at them. Nevertheless, they did have to endure three Russian winters in the far north of the country, the first with clothing little suited to the conditions.

The privations inflicted on the populace defy rational understanding. The fact that they were able to endure such hardships is both inspiring and heartbreaking. The death toll is simply incomprehensible. Ingenuity and forbearance go some way to explain how the people of Leningrad managed to hold out against such unimaginable hardships but could never fully explain how it was achieved.

This siege needs to be understood by anyone seeking to comprehend Russian resolve. There has long been a tendency to underestimate Russia's capabilities as a country. Their leadership can be woeful, obtuse and inept. Rampant corruption and stifling bureaucracy also hamper their ability to function. However, they have a clear advantage when it comes to endurance, and any country intent on testing their resolve needs to factor in the point that they will need to remain unflinchingly focussed on their goal for the long term.